# Learning to See

# Learning to See

Teaching American Sign Language
as a Second Language

SECOND EDITION

Sherman Wilcox and
Phyllis Perrin Wilcox

Gallaudet University Press    *Washington, D.C.*

Gallaudet University Press
Washington, D.C. 20002

Original edition published 1991 by the Center for
Applied Linguistics and Prentice-Hall, Inc. Second edition
published 1997 by Gallaudet University Press.

Printed in the United States of America

Library of Congress Cataloging-in-Publication Data

Wilcox, Sherman.
    Learning to see : teaching American sign language as a second language /
Sherman Wilcox and Phyllis Wilcox. — 2nd ed.
      p.     cm.
    Includes bibliographical references and index.
    ISBN 1-56368-059-9 (alk. paper)
    1. American Sign Language—Study and teaching.   2. Language teachers—
Training of—United States.   3. Second language acquisition—United
States.   I. Wilcox, Phyllis.
HV2474.W55    1996
419—dc20                                    96-30658
                                             CIP

Cover design by Shelley Gruendler
Interior design by Dennis Anderson
Composition by Wilsted & Taylor

*To the many wonderful American Sign Language students at the University of New Mexico who have enriched our lives as language teachers.*

# Contents

# *Preface*

Foreign language teachers often tell us that the goal of teaching a second language is to propel students beyond the limits of their own world, to encourage them to see through the language and culture of another people (Bugos 1980). Such a goal is entirely appropriate for teachers of American Sign Language (ASL). In the best language classrooms, students are treated to an extended voyage into a new and exciting world. They learn to talk about the familiar in unfamiliar ways, to consider values that may seem questionable.

ASL students, too, are exposed to a different world. They are learning a new language, one that is unlike anything they are likely to have experienced before. ASL is, in every sense of the word, a foreign language. ASL students are also encouraged to view the world through the eyes of a different culture. The Deaf[1] way of looking at the world is, as will be clear in this text, a foreign culture to second language students.

Ben Bahan, a noted ASL teacher and Deaf writer, has proposed that Deaf people start calling themselves "seeing people" (Bahan 1989b).

> By using that word I put myself in a position of things I can do, instead of what I can't do. Since I identified myself as a seeing person, that would explain everything around me: like TTYs,

decoders, flashing doorbells, lipreading, and the emergence of a seeing language, American Sign Language. (p. 32)

Entry into a foreign land is never easy. The first step must be to learn the language and culture of the people who live there. For students who wish to visit the world of Deaf people, ASL classes are the door—*learning to see* is the key.

The authors would like to thank Professor Deb Smith and Charles Wilkinson for their invaluable assistance, and Ivey Pittle Wallace and Jill Hendricks, our editors at Gallaudet University Press.

## Notes

1. In the literature on ASL and its users, it is common practice to use the term *deaf* to refer to the audiological condition of not being able to hear and the term *Deaf* to refer to the cultural group that uses ASL and shares other values and beliefs.

*Learning to See*

# 1

## More than a Gesture

### Introduction

In 1965, an event took place that was to change the history of a language and its people. William C. Stokoe, Dorothy Casterline, and Carl Croneberg published their *Dictionary of American Sign Language on Linguistic Principles*. At the time, few people paid attention. Although American Sign Language (ASL) was the language of a large population in this country, few hearing Americans knew it existed.

Fourteen years later, Edward Klima and Ursula Bellugi, linguists at the Salk Institute for Biological Studies in La Jolla, California, published *The Signs of Language*, the first in-depth description of the grammar of ASL. Still, relatively few people knew about ASL. Fewer still were able to study it as a second language. As of 1982, Battison and Carter wrote that "as far as we know, no college or university has yet made [American] Sign Language a permanent part of its foreign language curricula, on a par with the other foreign languages they teach" (p. vii).

By the mid-1980s, the scene had changed radically. ASL programs were being established on campuses and in high schools across the country. ASL could be seen everywhere: on television (for example, in *Barney Miller*, *Happy Days*, *Love Is Never Silent*, *Star Trek: The Next Generation*, and even a McDonald's commercial); in the theater (Mark Medoff's *Children of a Lesser God*); at the movies (*Voices*, a movie that generated much controversy in the Deaf

1

community because a hearing actress portrayed the part of a deaf woman, and the film version of *Children of a Lesser God*); at political rallies; in high school and college classrooms, where deaf students were mainstreamed with hearing students. ASL was beginning to pervade the American experience.

Interest in ASL has reached an all-time high and shows no signs of declining. No matter where we look, the situation is the same. As soon as one ASL course is established, there are enough students to fill two. If two classes are opened, enough students show up to fill four.

Any language teacher has to feel heartened by such popularity and acceptance of a previously neglected language, especially when it is a language in our very midst. For those who have been in the field of ASL for many years, it seems miraculous. Unfortunately, such rapid growth can also be dangerous. In their attempts to establish new ASL programs and to meet the ever-increasing demand for more classes, many schools are offering courses that do not really teach ASL; instead, they teach some version of Pidgin Sign English or a form of manually coded English. (We will discuss these terms in detail in the next chapter.) It would be hard even for traditional language courses to keep up with increasing enrollments of the magnitude experienced in ASL. The field of ASL instruction was, understandably, ill-prepared to respond. There were few teacher training programs; there was a paucity of materials, no standard curricula, little or no literature on second language instruction of ASL, and no accreditation procedures for ASL programs and teachers. It was common to find ASL being taught by well-intentioned instructors with far too little knowledge of the language and its users. There is little that a textbook alone can do for these teachers; one can only hope that the field will offer enough support to allow under-prepared teachers to become more competent.

Of course, many schools have been aware of this danger and have consistently maintained high standards in their ASL courses. The instructors in these courses are either native users of ASL or highly fluent second language users; they have degrees or experience in second language instruction; they use materials that are designed specifically for the teaching of ASL and not for some other form of signed language; and they associate on a regular basis with Deaf people. It is also common, however, to find good teachers who need program and classroom guidelines for the teaching of ASL. These teachers must learn how to teach their students about the history and structure of ASL. They must learn what materials are available and how to evaluate and use them; how to design and implement an ASL curriculum; how to develop effective teaching strategies, and evaluate students' performance; and how to incorporate Deaf culture into the ASL classroom. It is to these instructors that we offer our book.

There are two groups of people for whom this book is not intended. First, it is not directed to those who do not know ASL. If you are interested in teaching ASL and do not yet know the language, then your course is clear. Study ASL and get to know Deaf people. Spend several years becoming fluent; spend a few more learning about how to teach languages to second language students. You will be rewarded with excellent career opportunities. Second, this book is not intended for experienced ASL instructors who are familiar with most of the issues highlighted herein. Nonetheless, we encourage such readers to use this book as a reference source and to offer it to others who have less experience teaching ASL.

## Myths and Misconceptions about ASL

Many second language students are attracted to ASL courses because of a curiosity about the language and its users. Students do hold, however, many misconceptions about ASL. Unless these misconceptions are examined and dispelled, they will impede students' appreciation for and acquisition of ASL.

This section discusses some of the myths and misconceptions that pervade popular thinking about ASL, both as a human language and as a foreign or second language. We will examine these myths and misconceptions by posing the common questions that they lead people to ask.

## Is American Sign Language a Derivative of English?

Because of its signed modality, people often assume that ASL is merely a gestural representation of English. ASL is a fully developed, natural language, one of the world's many signed languages. It is not a derivative of English; ASL contains structures and processes that English does not (Klima and Bellugi 1979). Neither is it a *simplified* language. ASL is a complete language with its own unique grammar (Fromkin 1988). It is also a rich language with a long and interesting history. In order to appreciate ASL as a language independent from spoken and written languages, and from other signed languages, students should be taught the history and structure of ASL.

## Is ASL a System of Communication or a Language?

There are many ways to communicate information. Bees communicate the direction of flowers with an elaborate dance in which they wiggle their tails. Animals communicate information about territoriality by odor. Facial expressions, calls, and other systems of nonverbal communication are used by primates. Even single cells communicate information by means of DNA and the genetic code. All of these are *systems of communication* (Akmajian, Demers, and Harnish 1984). Human languages certainly share some features with these systems of communication; for example, they have a channel through which they are transmitted (auditory, visual, olfactory, chemical). However, human languages have features that set them apart from these more general systems of communication.

One of the most important of these features is *productivity*. Human languages are composed of a limited set of parts that can be combined to form a potentially unlimited set of structures. For example, sounds can be combined to form different words, and words can be combined to form an infinite number of sentences. This aspect of productivity manifests itself in two ways: production and comprehension. People can both produce and understand sentences never seen or heard before. It is unlikely, for example, that anyone has ever before seen the sentence, "During the hurricane, Marlon Brando spilled a hatful of chocolate soup on his blue suede shoes." Although the meaning is nonsensical, users of English would not fail to understand the words. In chapter 2, we will discuss productivity and its presence in signed languages such as ASL.

Human languages are also characterized by *arbitrariness* and *displacement*. Words in natural human languages do not necessarily resemble their referents (arbitrariness). The word *bear* is not a bear, nor does the word smell, sound, or look like the animal that it signifies. Humans can talk about things removed in time and space from their personal experience (displacement). They can talk about events that happened yesterday, or that might happen tomorrow. They can wonder about events happening across the world just as easily as they can remark about events taking place in front of them. They can talk about such concrete objects as cars or houses, or such abstract concepts as love, honesty, or God.

Thus, it is only partially true to say that human languages such as English or Spanish are systems of communication. They are that and more. The same is true for ASL. ASL is a system of communication, and it is more—it is a true human language, with all the features characteristic of other human languages. This means that an abstract concept can be expressed in ASL as easily as in English, Spanish, Navajo, or any other spoken language.

Perhaps one reason many people believe that ASL is merely a system of communication is that they have quite detailed—but largely incorrect—ideas about what constitutes a human language. For example, many people, including some language teachers and researchers, assume that all human languages are spoken. They also make assumptions about the relationship between speech and other forms of language, such as writing. On the basis of these preconceptions, people make reasonable but incorrect inferences about ASL.

## *Is ASL a More Conceptual Language than English?*

This is a common question. There seems to be something about ASL that makes people want to call it a "conceptual" language. In truth, though, it makes little sense to say that one language is more conceptual than another. All languages are conceptual; they package concepts into linguistic units of various sizes—words, phrases, sentences, texts—so that the concepts can be communicated to others.

The real question is not whether one language is more or less conceptual than another, but how a particular language chooses to package concepts. In some languages, Navajo for instance, a word may contain much more information than a typical English word. One word in Navajo may have to be translated into English as a phrase or even a sentence. This does not make Navajo more conceptual than English; the two languages merely have different ways of packaging concepts.

In fact, ASL is quite similar to Navajo in this regard. Much more information can be packed into a typical ASL sign than into a typical English word. Perhaps this is what people are noticing when they say that ASL is more conceptual than English.

Another feature of ASL that may have an influence on this question is that of arbitrariness. As explained, a universal characteristic of human languages is arbitrariness—in general, words do not resemble their referents. ASL, on the other hand, does seem to exhibit a high degree of iconicity—ASL words often seem to resemble features of their referent. A common example is the ASL word TREE (figure 1), which does indeed resemble a tree. The evolution of ASL over the last 75 to 100 years, however, is such that the degree of iconicity is decreasing (Frishberg 1975). Certain aspects of the grammar of ASL also work to suppress iconicity (Klima and Bellugi 1979).

Figure 1: TREE

*Source:* Reprinted, by permission of the publisher, from E. Shroyer, *Signs of the Times* (Washington, D.C.: Gallaudet University Press, 1982), 24.

Even spoken languages incorporate some iconicity. Sound symbolism is one example: words like *choo-choo* and *cockadoodledoo.* Woodworth (1991) finds an iconic relationship between vowel pitch and distance in deictic pronouns and place adverbs in 26 languages chosen from a worldwide sample.

Written languages at various stages in their development also exhibit a degree of iconicity. Many students are familiar with the early history of writing, in which written symbols clearly resembled elements of the real world. As writing systems evolved, they typically lost their iconic elements and became more conventionalized and arbitrary.

Finally, the degree to which any language incorporates arbitrariness and iconicity is open to much debate. We have considered cases of iconicity only at the word level, where words or signs can resemble their referents. There are many other places that iconicity can appear in language. When examining these other areas, we find that ASL may be no more or less iconic than spoken languages (Haiman 1985).

It would be nice to be able to claim that ASL is a more conceptual language than English; this would possibly allay many people's fear that ASL is a simplified language. Neither position is true.

*Is ASL a Universal Language?*

No. ASL is indigenous to the United States and parts of Canada. There are many naturally occurring, indigenous signed languages in the world, just as there are many natural spoken languages. Just as people who speak English cannot understand people who speak Chinese, people (whether they are deaf or hearing) who know ASL cannot understand people who use Chinese Sign Language.

It is interesting that most people assume that sign language is universal. Perhaps this is because many people wrongly assume that sign language is based on universal emotional expressions or body language. This is not the case. In fact, research on young deaf children with deaf parents has demonstrated that these children make a clear distinction between the use of facial expressions to convey emotions and facial expressions to convey grammatical features of the language (McIntire and Reilly 1988).

People may also assume that ASL is not a naturally-occurring language but was instead devised by hearing people to help deaf people understand and acquire language. Why, they wonder, would people devise more than one signed language? The answer, of course, is that no one invented ASL; it is a naturally-occurring language. They may be confusing ASL with one of several manual codes for English, which will be discussed later.

When people learn that ASL is not universal, they often remark, "Wouldn't it be nice if deaf people all over the world could communicate with each other?" Perhaps it would. It might also be nice if hearing people the world over could break language barriers. The fact is that people everywhere use different languages, and deaf people are no exception. It is also true that people acquire a sense of identity, a sense of pride, through the language they use. Again, deaf people are no exception. As will be shown in chapter 4, the use of and respect for ASL is a major avenue to admission into Deaf culture.

## Is ASL a "Foreign" Language?

The question of whether ASL is "foreign" depends on the specific meaning of "foreign." If several people were asked what qualifies as a foreign language, most would probably respond, "a language used in another country." The foreignness of the language is directly related to whether or not it is associated with a geopolitical entity—a foreign nationality different from our own. But, the matter is not so simple. Consider the case of Navajo. Some universities in the United States teach Navajo and accept it in fulfillment of their undergraduate foreign language requirement. Yet, Navajo clearly does not originate in a foreign country—like many other languages, Navajo is indigenous to the United States. Many of the world's languages are not affiliated with nationalities and thus, under this definition, would not be considered foreign languages. Not only would this definition lead to an untenable position on the status of these languages as foreign languages, it would fail to explain some of the most important events taking place in our world today. Much of the current restructuring of the world, especially in the former Soviet bloc countries, is motivated by ethnic unrest. Much of the sense of ethnic identity derives from the use of a particular language.

Furthermore, many of the languages taught as foreign languages at American universities actually have a long history of use in this country. Spanish is an obvious example. Spanish is the native language of many United States citizens who do not consider themselves foreigners. In spite of this, almost every school in the country that has a foreign language requirement accepts Spanish in fulfillment of that requirement.

Alternatively, consider the special situation of foreign exchange students in the United States. They come here speaking both their mother tongue and English. Which is their foreign language? Clearly, it is not the language that originates in another country; it is not their native language. If anything, English is their foreign language.

Foreign language requirements are designed to move students to learn a language that they do not already know—a language that is foreign to them and to their experience. ASL qualifies admirably as foreign in this sense. For this reason, many language scholars now speak of second language, rather than foreign language, requirements.

Issues related to the acceptance of ASL as a foreign language are being debated in school districts, universities, and state legislatures across the country. ASL teachers and students should be aware of the movement to accept ASL as a foreign language and should be prepared to discuss the issues with others. Some of these issues are presented in more detail in chapter 2.

## American Deaf Culture

Every language student knows there is more involved in a second language course than just learning a new language. Students must also learn about the culture of the people who use the language. The same is true for second language students of ASL. They should learn about the culture of American Deaf people.

For many people, the idea that there is such a thing as American Deaf culture is new. ASL instructors must be prepared to teach their students about the values and beliefs of Deaf people and to help students understand the concept of culture as it applies to deafness.

There are many ways in which ASL students can learn about Deaf culture, both explicitly and implicitly. Chapter 3 presents information about Deaf culture that can be shared with ASL students in an explicit way. Teachers can also bring Deaf culture into the classroom implicitly by the way they structure the classroom, the lessons, and the materials. Of course, the best way for students to learn about Deaf culture, and to learn ASL for that matter, is for the teacher to be Deaf. This is not always possible, however. In these circumstances, hearing teachers can directly

expose students to Deaf culture by inviting Deaf people to participate in class sessions and by encouraging ASL students to seek out
Deaf people in the local community. These and other strategies
will be discussed in chapter 4.

## The Plan of the Book

Chapter 2 describes ASL in more detail, including its history and structure. The text includes more discussion of the linguistics of ASL than may be typical in a book on second language
learning because of the number of linguistic and cultural issues
that must be explained to the student of ASL as a second language.
We begin our discussion of this by highlighting the following
three points.

- Because ASL has only recently been studied as a legitimate first
  or second language, much information about the language
  comes directly from linguistic research. Teachers and students
  must be able to use and understand this information in order to
  pursue their study of ASL.
- Whereas ASL is a language like any other, it is also a special
  type of language—a *signed* language. When dealing with signed
  languages, people cannot assume that teaching the language
  itself is sufficient. Students must not merely be able to converse
  fluently in ASL; they must also understand the nature of signed
  languages in general and their relationship to spoken and written forms of language.
- Second language students will often serve as provisional ambassadors for ASL. Part of the reason for this is the aforemen-
  tioned great popularity and curiosity regarding ASL. Of course,
  it would be best if people satisfied their desire to learn more
  about ASL by taking a course from a Deaf person. The reality is,
  however, that when looking for sources of information, many
  people will turn to friends or colleagues who have studied ASL.
  In addition to acquiring communicative competence in ASL,
  students must also acquire a healthy respect for and under-

standing of the language, its structure, its history, and its users. Students must be able to talk competently about signed languages in general and, more specifically, about ASL to others.

Chapter 3 presents information about the Deaf community and Deaf culture. Chapter 4 discusses issues related to ASL instruction. Finally, chapter 5 explores some of the special issues facing ASL instructors: (1) introducing ASL students to the Deaf community and to native users of ASL; (2) ASL teacher qualifications; and (3) the important difference between people who can communicate fluently (using ASL) with Deaf people, and those who have the additional language and professional skills required to be interpreters for Deaf people.

# 2
# American Sign Language in Perspective

## A Short History of ASL

American Sign Language (ASL) is the visual/gestural language that serves as the primary means of communication of deaf people in the United States and parts of Canada. It is difficult to extrapolate the size of the deaf population because the United States Bureau of the Census has not included a question on hearing loss since the national survey in 1930. In 1974 the National Association of the Deaf, in cooperation with the Deafness Research and Training Center at New York University, conducted a special census of the deaf population. There has been a lack of consensus regarding the definition of deafness and how to determine who is deaf or hard of hearing. The National Center for Health Statistics estimates that there are perhaps 20 million persons with a hearing loss, with approximately 550,000 persons with the "inability to hear and understand speech" (Holt and Hotto 1994, 2). In 1987, Padden estimated that between 100,000 and 500,000 people use ASL. This estimate included native signers who learned ASL as their first language from deaf parents, hearing children of deaf parents who also learned ASL as their native language, and fluent signers who have learned ASL from deaf people. In the past decade, thousands of additional students in universities and educational settings have begun acquiring ASL. The number of ASL users continues to grow yearly.

The history of ASL is long and rich. Much of its early development, however, remains poorly documented. One reason for this is that, as in the case of spoken languages, the early forms of signed languages are not preserved. Research can establish the time and circumstances under which education and formal instruction in English and in various forms of signing were brought to deaf people in the United States, but little is known about the structure of the language that deaf people used prior to this. Despite the paucity of information about earlier forms of signed language, one should not doubt that deaf people did communicate with each other in a natural signed language even before hearing people began to take an interest in deaf education. There are two sources of evidence that indicate deaf people used natural signed languages before hearing people intervened.

## Natural Signed Languages Before ASL

### Vineyard Sign Language

The first source of evidence is the unique situation that developed on Martha's Vineyard in the late seventeenth century (Groce 1985). Martha's Vineyard is an island five miles off the southeastern shore of Massachusetts. From 1690 to the mid-twentieth century, a high rate of genetic deafness appeared in the island population. Whereas the normal incidence rate for deafness in the population of nineteenth-century America was approximately 1 out of every 5,700 people, the incidence on Martha's Vineyard was 1 out of every 155. In some areas of the island, the ratio was even higher; in one town, for example, 1 in every 25 people was born deaf, and in a certain neighborhood the ratio was as high as one in four.

Martha's Vineyard was an excellent example of a strong and flourishing deaf community. Of particular interest is the evidence of an indigenous signed language used on the island. The first deaf islander, who arrived with his wife and family in 1692, was fluent in some type of signed language. Many of the families that inhabited the island had moved there from the Boston area; before this they had immigrated from a region in England known as the

Weald, in the county of Kent. Almost all of the deaf inhabitants of Martha's Vineyard could trace their ancestry back to this small, isolated area in England.

As the deaf community on Martha's Vineyard flourished, so did their language. One can only surmise that this local signed language was based on a regional variety of British sign language. Soon, it spread in use to the entire island so that almost every individual, deaf or hearing, was able to use the Vineyard sign language. The impact on deaf people, according to Groce, must have been tremendous. With much of the hearing population of the island bilingual in spoken English and Vineyard sign language, deafness was not viewed as a handicap. Deaf people were full participants in all aspects of island society (Groce 1985).

### A Signed Language in Eighteenth-Century France

The second story providing evidence that deaf people had their own natural signed languages before hearing people became involved in the lives of the deaf comes from the French Enlightenment (Lane 1984).

In 1779, a deaf Parisian bookbinder, Pierre Desloges, wrote a book, *Observations of a Deaf-Mute,* describing the signed language used by deaf Parisians. Desloges felt compelled to write his book, he said, because at the time a certain Abbé Deschamps was proclaiming that signed languages could not be considered languages, and thus were of no use in the education of young deaf children. Learning of this, Desloges felt he must speak on behalf of the natural signed language of French deaf people. "Like a Frenchman who sees his language belittled by a German who only knows a few French words, I thought I was obliged to defend my language against the false charges of this author" (Moody 1987, 301).

The situation that Desloges described should not surprise us. Deaf people in France did indeed have a natural signed language (we will call it Old French Sign Language [OFSL]) that they used to discuss all type of matters—politics, work, religion, family, and so forth.[1] This language was passed down from deaf person to deaf person, much as any language that is not popularly accepted in educational institutions is transmitted to younger generations of speakers. Describing the typical deaf youth in eighteenth-century France, Desloges wrote the following:

> He meets deaf-mutes more knowledgeable than himself, he learns to combine and perfect his signs . . . he quickly acquires, in interactions with his comrades, the so "difficult"—so they say!—art of expressing and painting one's thoughts, even the most abstract, by means of natural signs and with as much order and precision as if he knew all the rules of grammar. (Moody 1987, 301)

Clearly, Desloges is describing what any second language teacher would call syntax (order) and pronunciation (precision).

It was a young cleric in Paris, the Abbé de l'Épée, who first recognized that signed language could be used to educate deaf children. Visiting the home of a local parishioner, Épée noticed two young deaf daughters signing to each other. One can assume that, as Desloges wrote, these sisters were using OFSL and were on their way to becoming enculturated into Deaf French society.

The Abbé de l'Épée was moved by what he saw. He learned from the girls' mother that the only education they were receiving was private tutoring by means of pictures. From this inauspicious beginning, Épée went on to found the first free educational institution for deaf people in France in 1771.

Épée did realize that signed language could be used to educate deaf children, but apparently he did not realize that OFSL was a fully developed, natural language. Instead, he immediately set about modifying the signed language that his pupils taught him. He devised signs to represent all the verb endings, articles, prepositions, and auxiliary verbs present in spoken French.

> Thus, for example, the word "believe" was analyzed as the sum of "know" plus "feel" plus "say" plus "not see" and it was signed by executing the corresponding four signs and that for "verb." (Lane 1980, 122)

These historical developments in the evolution of signed language in France are quite significant, and, in principle, they are repeated in nineteenth- and twentieth-century American deaf education. The language of the French deaf community, Old French Sign Language, was a natural signed language that functioned admirably in all aspects of community life. Educators, with the most benevolent of intentions, saw OFSL as lacking in grammar. Of course, OFSL did not lack grammar; it merely had a different grammar than French because OFSL and French were two different languages. In an effort to bolster what were seen as inadequacies in the language, educators such as Épée modified it to make it look more like a signed form of French (we would call it *Old Signed French*). It was this heavily modified and slightly invented language that was taught to young deaf French children. Presumably, then, there were two languages in the Paris school: the artificial system that Épée invented (Old Signed French), used in the classroom; and OFSL, used by deaf children and adults in their informal interactions.

## ASL in America—The French Connection

France is important not only because it provides us with evidence that natural signed languages existed, but also because the development that took place in France had a direct bearing on the development of ASL in this country. By the early nineteenth century, when the Paris school had been taken over by Épée's successor, Roch Ambroise Sicard, former teachers and students from the Paris school had gone on to establish several schools in France. Teachers and students from the Paris school made regular tours across Europe demonstrating their methods. In 1816, a young Protestant minister and recent graduate of Yale, Thomas Hopkins Gallaudet, became interested in educating deaf children. Wanting to learn all that he could about teaching methods, he undertook a trip to Europe.

Gallaudet first traveled to England, where the predominant approach in deaf education was the oral method, an approach that emphasized the development of speech. While in London, Gallaudet met a group of teachers and students, including Sicard and Laurent Clerc, a brilliant young deaf man and recent graduate of the Paris school. Gallaudet traveled to Paris with them and studied deaf education methods and signed language with Clerc.

Eventually, Gallaudet convinced Clerc to return to America with him to establish what became the first permanent American school for the deaf—the American Asylum at Hartford, Connecticut. On the voyage from France to America, Clerc and Gallaudet adapted the signed language used at the Paris school to meet what they perceived to be the needs of deaf children in America.

There is evidence that Clerc was not only fluent in OFSL and Old Signed French, but also highly literate in French. It is likely that the language Clerc taught Gallaudet was actually the modified system of signs that had been developed to teach French to deaf children (that is, Old Signed French). The modifications Clerc and Gallaudet made were to adapt it to the grammar of English: Signs were invented for English verb endings, articles, prepositions, etc. Thus, what Gallaudet and Clerc brought to American deaf education was an early form of *Signed English* based on the lexical forms of Old Signed French, which was itself based on OFSL.

When they arrived in America, Gallaudet and Clerc began using their signed language in the classroom. In writings of the time, this system of signing was called *methodical signs*. It was not long before teachers began to note that although the students used methodical signs—what we will call Old Signed English—in the classroom, they used another type of signed language in their interactions with each other. Gallaudet (1819, quoted in Lane 1980) wrote the following:

> A successful teacher of the deaf and dumb should be thoroughly acquainted both with their own peculiar mode of expressing their ideas by signs and also with that of expressing the same ideas by those methodical signs that in their arrangement correspond to the structure of written language. For the natural language of this singular class of beings has its appropriate style and structure. They use it in their unrestrained communication with each other, [it is marked by] great abruptness, ellipses, and inversion of expression . . . To take a familiar example . . . "You must not eat that fruit, it will make you feel unwell" . . . In [the deaf's] own language of

signs, literally translated, it would be thus, "Fruit that you eat, you unwell, you eat no." (p. 126)

Gallaudet's recognition that the deaf had their own "natural language" was to be commended; however, it seems that, like Épée, he too failed to understand fully that this language was an independent, grammatical language. Gallaudet encouraged teachers to respect and learn this way of communicating, but he still insisted on comparing its structure to English and then noting that it is marked by ellipsis (leaving out words) and inversion of expression (presumably, the fact that this language did not follow English word order). One may speculate that if Gallaudet had commented on Russian, he would have noted that it is marked by ellipsis because it does not have articles. If he had commented on Latin, he would have claimed that it too is marked by inversion of expression because the word order in Latin is freer than that in English.

This "natural signing" is Old American Sign Language. Researchers may never know whether there was a commonly accepted variety or a high degree of local variation. The fact is clear, however, that the early methodical signs with their heritage in Old French Sign Language began to mix with the indigenous language that was already being used by deaf people in America. The result is known today as ASL.

In the century and three-quarters since these two languages first came into contact, there has been much development. Near the turn of the twentieth century, people feared that the predominant oral method would snuff out both languages. In a particularly moving speech recorded on silent film in 1913, George W. Veditz, president of the National Association of the Deaf, made an emotional plea for all Deaf people to cherish and preserve their beloved signed languages as "the noblest gift God has given to the Deaf."

Today, linguists estimate that, for a sample of 872 modern ASL and FSL words, the percentage of cognates may be as great as 58 percent (Lane 1987). Modern British Sign Language and ASL, on the other hand, are almost mutually incomprehensible.

## The Linguistics of ASL

One lesson to be learned from this brief history of ASL is that even those who are familiar with signed languages and who have the best interests of deaf students at heart can be sadly mistaken in their views of signed language. The myths and misconceptions raised in chapter 1 demonstrate that these same mistaken views are still prevalent today; there is much that instructors need to know about ASL if they are to teach it to others. ASL instructors must understand that second language students arrive in the classroom filled with misconceptions. Much of the process of learning ASL, at least in the early stages, is not just learning the language but *unlearning* what is already presupposed about the language.

For this reason, ASL instructors need a firm understanding of some basic linguistic concepts regarding ASL. Knowing the structure of language in the way that linguists think about language is one of the best ways to clarify our students' thinking about ASL. There are other reasons, however, for teachers to possess a working knowledge of ASL linguistics. First, ASL does not have the long heritage of language instruction enjoyed by other languages. Much of what is known about ASL comes directly from state-of-the-art research conducted by ASL linguists; often, several years pass before this research begins to appear in textbooks. ASL teachers need to be able to obtain their information from the source. In order to do this, they need at least a working knowledge of ASL linguistics.

Second, as mentioned in the introduction, students of ASL often become ambassadors for the language. In order to explain to others what ASL is and is not, teachers and students need to know how to talk about languages, how to compare and contrast languages in different modalities, and how to describe languages that deviate from our traditional understanding. It is as difficult to explain how ASL is different from English as it is to explain how a non-Indo-European language such as Navajo is different from English. Most students, if they are familiar with another language at all, are probably familiar with one that is structurally similar to English. When they become interested in a language such as ASL, which is quite unlike any language in their prior experience, it is a special challenge for instructors to convey to them its uniqueness.

Third, concepts can be borrowed and adapted from linguistics and used effectively in the ASL classroom. For example, students in spoken language classrooms have available to them a concept that is quite useful in their acquisition of a second language—the concept of pronunciation. Simply having the term *pronunciation* is a tremendous cognitive tool for spoken language students. ASL students, on the other hand, frequently have to rely on several varying and rather subjective ways of talking about how they produce ASL—their "pronunciation." By borrowing from ASL linguistics, teachers can introduce to students the concepts of ASL phonology, the components of ASL words, and thus give them a tool to think about and focus on their pronunciation of ASL.

## The Language/Mode Distinction

The first step in understanding ASL and how it compares and contrasts with other languages is to understand what we will call the *language/mode distinction*. The concept is simple: There are languages, and there are modalities or channels for producing languages. The three major channels discussed here are the spoken, written, and signed channels (Baron 1981). They are shown in figure 2.

The spoken channel is the one most familiar to us—it is the primary channel for most of the world's languages. By primary, we mean that spoken languages are independent in the sense that they directly represent concepts; they do not rely on another representational system for their meaning.

The picture writing system of the New Mexico Pueblo Indians did not present symbols for sounds in association with any one language. Carol Patterson-Rudolph (1993) claims that the Pueblo rock writing is not simply a form of art open to artistic interpretation, but is cross-linguistic, much in the same way that ideas are transmitted through a symbolic (signed) language that bypasses the verbal language specific to any one tribe. Thus, various Indian groups can interpret, to some degree, the general messages "written" by the petroglyphs found on rocks.

The written modality, on the other hand, can be either a primary or secondary modality. Sampson (1985), for instance, gives an example of a written language that is not parasitic on speech. It is a letter sent by a girl of the Yukaghir tribe of northeastern Siberia to a young man. The letter itself looks like a stylized, abstractionist painting. Sampson demonstrates, however, that the letter contains specific content; the interpretation of the letter is dissimilar to an interpretation of a painting, the former has a detailed and precise meaning.

Examples of this sort are extremely rare. In general, the written modality is secondary. Writing is a secondary representation of speech; it is a representation of a representation. It is not naturally occurring in the same sense that speech is. People can and do devise writing systems for previously unwritten languages. Considered in terms of the numbers of speakers, the most used languages in the world are written languages: Chinese, Arabic, English, and so forth. Considered in terms of the number of languages in the world, however, languages that have a written form

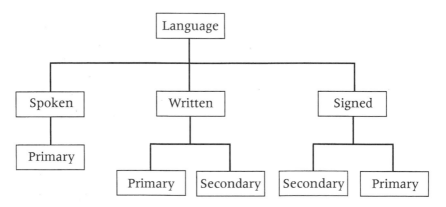

Figure 2: Language/Mode Distinction

are the exception. Most of the world's languages are unwritten languages.

What about the signed modality? It would be reasonable to assume that the signed modality functions exactly like the written modality; that, except for rare instances, it is a secondary modality for representing naturally-occurring spoken languages. This seems to be what people think when they assume that ASL is really just English. It is a reasonable assumption: People *speak and write* the same language in this country (English), so why isn't it the case that when they *sign,* it is also the same language? There is a long tradition of assuming that speech is the primary modality for representing language, and that therefore speech is synonymous with language. There exists an equally long tradition that recognizes writing as a secondary system. It is little wonder, then, that when people first encounter the signed modality, they assume that the relationship between speech and sign is the same as that between speech and writing.

This is not the case. More correctly, it is only partially the case. The signed modality can function as either the primary or the secondary modality for conveying language. In the former case, an entire class of natural languages occurs in the signed modality: signed languages. As naturally-occurring languages, these signed languages are unrelated to spoken languages. They stand in various types of relationships to each other, as do spoken languages. When they occur in the same geographic locality as a particular spoken language, they may also influence or be influenced by that spoken language.

In the latter case, the signed modality can, in fact, function in the same manner as the written modality. The signed modality can be used to devise a secondary representation system for speech. When the signed modality is used to represent English, the resulting systems are called *manual codes for English* (MCE). MCE will be discussed in more detail in a later section of this chapter. For now, it is important to recognize that the signed modality functions as a primary means of conveying languages.

Signed languages do not depend on other languages or other modalities—they are fully independent human languages.

Naming a particular modality does not name a language. Many languages can be represented in the spoken modality. All speech is not English. English is more than speech; it is also writing. In talking about and teaching signed languages such as ASL, people often do not recognize this. Consider the following three scenarios.

A person walks into a large lecture hall filled with students. He starts to speak a language totally unknown to anyone in the hall. This is not a language such as German, Spanish, or Russian—a language that people can at least recognize even if they cannot speak or understand it. This is a very different language. Unsettled, one student, call her Sally, leans over, to her friend Susan and asks, "What is that?" Susan replies, "That's speech."

Sally would never accept this as an answer to her question. She has asked Susan what the person was speaking, not whether the person was speaking. Susan could argue that Sally's question was ambiguous. Sally would probably respond that Susan was being disingenuous. Sally could tell that the person was speaking—she wanted to know what language it was.

Consider the same situation with regard to writing. Suppose that a person walks into another large lecture hall and starts writing some cryptic language on the board. Sally again leans over to Susan and asks, "What is that?" Still her perverse self, Susan replies, "That's writing."

Again, one understands that Susan has not answered the proper question. The fact that someone is writing is obvious; Sally wants to know what *language* is being written. The problem with Susan's answers lies in the fact that speaking and writing name different modalities, not languages. Sally is looking for the name of a *language*, not the name of a *modality*.

Yet, consider this same situation for a signed language such as ASL. A Deaf person walks into the lecture hall and starts signing. Sally leans over and asks Susan, "What's that?" Susan replies, "That's sign language!"

Although Susan's answer, in this case, may seem satisfactory for the person who has never seen any signed language, in fact, it is no more helpful than her responses, "That's speech" or "That's writing." In all three situations, Susan answered the question of which *mode* was demonstrated—speech, writing, or signing— whereas she should have answered the question of which *language* was used.

The words people use often constrain the way they understand. Using the term *sign language* seems to imply that *sign* is a language. (See, for example, the otherwise excellent *Seeing Voices* by Oliver Sacks [1989], in which he uses the term *Sign* to refer to signed languages in general and ASL in particular.) It is important for students to understand and remember that signing is merely one way to produce a particular language, just as speaking is another way of producing languages. *Sign language* is no more a particular language than spoken language is. People do not speak *spoken language;* they speak particular spoken languages, such as Greek, Spanish, or German. The distinction is quite important. Although the term *sign language* may serve as a convenient short cut for referring to American Sign Language, it is dangerous because it so readily invites students to ignore this distinction. For this reason, we prefer to use the general term *signed language* when we are not referring to one particular language.

Languages stand in relation to other languages. The fact that several languages are listed in the left-hand column of table 1 implies that these languages are different from each other. English is not French; Navajo is not Chinese; Italian is not Spanish. By the same token, French Sign Language (FSL) is not British Sign Language (BSL); Chinese Sign Language (CSL) is not ASL; and ASL is not the same as FSL or BSL. They are all different languages.

Yet, different spoken languages may be related to each other. Consider Spanish and Italian. People who know Spanish can understand some Italian. This is not because Spanish is just "bad Italian." It is not because they are both spoken languages. Rather, it is because Spanish and Italian are historically related to each

Table 1. Language/Mode Relationships

| Language | Mode | | |
|---|---|---|---|
| | Spoken | Written | Signed |
| English | x | x | x |
| Italian | x | x | x |
| Spanish | x | x | x |
| Navajo | x | x | |
| French | x | x | x |
| American Sign Language | | x[a] | x |
| French Sign Language | | | x |
| British Sign Language | | | x |
| Chinese Sign Language | | | x |

[a]Although systems have been developed to write ASL, they are not in general use in the Deaf community.

other; they are both Romance languages. Likewise, English and French are related to each other because of historical circumstances such as the Norman Invasion.

The same is true for signed languages. Signed languages have various historical and familial relationships with each other. Students often ask, for example, which language is the closest relative to ASL. It would be reasonable for them to assume that it is BSL because so many of our ancestors came to America from Great Britain, and American English and British English are still closely related.

As shown in the previous section, however, this assumption is not correct. ASL's closest relative is not BSL; rather it is FSL. As for the case of English and French, the relationship between these two signed languages can be traced to historical circumstances— the meeting of Gallaudet and Clerc and their establishment of the first American school for the deaf in Hartford.

Finally, table 1 highlights the relationships among the three modalities. For example, English is both spoken and written; and, in the case of manual codes for English, it can be signed. Some languages spend much of their history represented in only one modality, such as speech. Later, writing systems may be invented and imposed on them. Navajo is such a language. Until very recently, Navajo was an unwritten language. An orthography for

Navajo was devised by Dr. Robert Young and introduced in the 1940s. Thus, unlike such languages as French, Spanish, Greek, and English, which have longstanding written traditions, the Navajo written tradition is quite young. It is uncertain whether the tradition will take root and flourish. Perhaps within another 50 years, the writing of Navajo will have died out. As it is, instruction in written Navajo is restricted to a few school programs.

Clearly, ASL is a signed language; it cannot be spoken. Can ASL be written? As a matter of fact, it can. Several writing systems have been devised by linguists and others (Newkirk 1987; Stokoe, Casterline, and Croneberg 1965; Sutton 1981). Like written Navajo, these writing systems are fairly recent inventions. They have not yet been used to create a literary tradition of written works in ASL. An example of one such writing system, SignFont (Newkirk 1987), is given here.

Ⓗ   ⋔h⊐llⁱⱽ•Ollⁱ⋔ (ρΦⁱⱽ•) ⎇ℚ⟩ᴹ.
ⅠσᵀX⟩X ⋔σⱽℽ⁼ ⋒⧟⌐XⱯℽ Ο•ΦⵔΦXℽᴹ

How is it that signed words can be written? In order to understand this, one must delve even further into the linguistics of ASL, in particular, into how words are formed in ASL.

*Words in a Signed Language: ASL Phonology*

Words are a good place to start our exploration of ASL linguistics. Words are at the heart of any language. When people learn a second language, they feel that it is important to learn vocabulary. Of course, there is much more to knowing a second language than vocabulary alone. Learners must know how to speak the words properly, how to make sentences, and how to accomplish things in the language (ask questions, provide information, carry on a conversation with a friend). They should also know the nature and customs of the people who use the language.

It is strange, then, that in regard to ASL, people rarely talk of learning words. Instead, they talk of learning signs, as if signs were somehow different from words. They are not. Whether they are spoken, written, or signed, words are the basic building block of languages. We do not use different names for spoken as opposed to written words (we could call written words *writes,* for example). Perhaps for our students this confusing terminology should be dropped; we should start calling signed words what they are— words.

What is a word? For linguists, there are various ways of looking at this question. On one level, words are symbols. Symbols are units that combine two entities: X symbolizes Y. Because they are symbols, all words have two poles: They are combinations of forms (usually taken to mean sounds) and meanings. Thus, the English word *cat* has a spoken form, written in phonetic transcription as /kæt/, and a meaning (a small, furry household pet is one possible meaning). The study of the form of words is called *phonetics* and *phonology;* the study of the meaning is called *semantics.*

Sometimes researchers analyze words only on the form side. Even here, words are made up of parts. At this level, of course, the parts do not mean anything because only one side of the symbol has been considered. For spoken words, this is the level of sounds. Looking again at the English word *cat,* one finds that the word is made of three parts: the sounds /k/, /æ/, and /t/. Linguists call these units *phonemes.*

There are other ways that linguists analyze words, ways that cannot be fully discussed here. For example, words may be analyzed in terms of rhythmic units called *syllables.* The English word *curriculum* has four syllables. Other, far more esoteric units have been posited by linguists in their efforts to understand spoken languages. The point for those interested in teaching and learning ASL is this: If ASL is a true human language, it can be analyzed by the same techniques used for spoken languages. What are words in ASL? Are they composed of the same basic parts as spoken words? How can a language without sounds, a signed language, have the same pieces as a spoken language?

### Three Stages in Our Understanding of ASL Phonology

To repeat a point made earlier, a critical feature of words is that they can be analyzed: Words consist of parts. For many years,

Figure 3: LIKE

*Source:* Reprinted, by permission of the publisher, from L. Lane, *Gallaudet Survival Guide to Signing* (Washington, D.C.: Gallaudet University Press, 1987), 102.

Figure 4: CHINESE

*Source:* Reprinted, by permission of the author, from E. Costello, *Signing: How to Speak with Your Hands* (New York: Bantam Books, 1983), 130.

people looked at signed languages and concluded that they were obviously different from spoken languages. Researchers claimed that signs, unlike words, are holistic (see, for example, Wundt 1921). These signs, people said, cannot be analyzed into parts that are then combined to form words. A gesture such as the sign LIKE (see figure 3) was considered an unanalyzable whole unit.

In the early 1960s, this conception of signed languages was challenged by the seminal work of William C. Stokoe (1960). Stokoe proposed that signs, in particular ASL signs, could indeed be analyzed into parts. According to Stokoe, ASL words could be broken down into three parameters—the handshape, the location, and the movement. Later, ASL researchers described a fourth parameter—the orientation of the palm of the hand.

How can one prove that these pieces of signs are indeed the equivalent to pieces of spoken words? One way is to use the technique upon which linguists have relied, the study of minimal pairs. In spoken languages, one can determine whether two sounds or phonemes contrast by substituting one for the other. For example, in the word *cat* (/kæt/), one could substitute the sound /b/ for the /k/: /bæt/. This does make a difference: *Cat* and *bat* are two different English words. Furthermore, the /b/ can be used in other words: *bad, ball,* etc.

Figure 5: X-Handshape

*Source:* Reprinted, by permission of the publisher, from L. Lane, *Gallaudet Survival Guide to Signing* (Washington, D.C.: Gallaudet University Press, 1987), ix.

This technique can be applied to signed words as well. Consider the word CHINESE[2] (figure 4). It consists of a handshape, labeled for the sake of convenience by ASL linguists as G; a location (the side of the eye on the same side of the face as the dominant hand); and a movement (a twisting or supinating movement of the forearm). It is possible to substitute these parts, or *parameters* as they are commonly referred to in the ASL linguistic literature. Let us take just the handshape parameter. Another handshape used in ASL is the X-handshape (figure 5). By substituting the X-handshape for the G-handshape in CHINESE, the signer produces the ASL word ONION; a change in one parameter (the X- versus the C-handshape) has indeed made a new ASL word.

At first, these pieces of signed words were called *cheremes* (taken from the Greek word *kheir* for *hand)* by analogy with phonemes. Notice that if we abstract from the two modalities, spoken and signed, we see that phonemes and cheremes are equivalent— they are the smallest building blocks of words that are recombined to form all the words of the language.

Thus, spoken words and signed words share an important characteristic: They are both formed by the combination of smaller units. Linguists have noted an interesting difference between the two modalities. The difference is in the way these units are combined.

Once again, take the case of the spoken word *cat.* The three phonemes in *cat* are combined in a specific temporal sequence: first /k/, then /æ/, and finally /t/. In only that particular sequence do these three phonemes make the word *cat*. In fact, if they are combined in a different sequence, they make a different word— /tæk/ *tack*, for example, or /ækt/ *act*.

This is not the case for cheremes. The component parts of signed words are not produced sequentially. It does not make sense, for example, to say that in the ASL word CHINESE the hand-shape is made first, and then the location, and finally the movement. Notice also that the parts cannot be recombined in a different sequence to obtain new ASL words. It is not possible to make one ASL word by first making a C, then the side-of-the-eye location, and then the supinating movement, and then a second ASL word by first making the location, then the movement, and lastly the handshape. All of these parts of ASL words are simultaneously present in the words.

Linguists soon took note of the fact that the phonology of spoken languages seemed to be characterized by a high degree of sequentiality whereas signed languages seemed to exhibit a high degree of simultaneity. They even offered explanations for this. Spoken languages, they claimed, are highly sequential because they rely on the acoustic channel, and sounds lend themselves to sequential transmission. Signed languages, on the other hand, are highly simultaneous because they rely on the optical channel, and light lends itself to simultaneous transmission (Bellugi and Studdert-Kennedy 1980).

Signed words and spoken words are both alike and different. They are alike because they consist of parts (phonemes or cheremes) that can be combined to form new words. This fact demonstrates that signed and spoken languages share a basic feature unique to all human languages. Signed and spoken languages differ, though, in the way in which they combine these parts. In signed languages, the formational components are combined simultaneously, whereas for spoken languages the components are strung together sequentially. This fact demonstrates the effect of modality on human language. Klima and Bellugi (1979) summarize the argument in the following manner:

> Thus the lexical items of ASL and all other primary sign languages we know of appear to be constituted in a different way from those of spoken languages: the organization of signs is primarily simultaneous rather than sequential. ASL uses a spatial medium; and this may crucially influence its organization. (p. 39)

There is a third and final stage in the history of our understanding of ASL words. In the late 1970s and early 1980s, ASL linguists began to propose that the phonology of ASL does incorporate sequentiality. Signs move to and from locations. They are characterized by periods of movement and lack of movement. In this stage of ASL history, linguists began to propose that the sequential production of a signed word's components did indeed need to be represented in the phonology of signed languages. In one popular analysis of ASL words, the periods of time in which the hands are moving are called *movements,* and the periods during which the hands do not move are called *holds* (Liddell 1984; Liddell and Johnson 1989).

The traditional, simultaneous analysis of ASL words did recognize that signs incorporate sequential characteristics. It did not, however, accord sequentiality a role in the phonology of ASL. Under the new analysis, signs are sequentially segmented into phonologically significant units, such as movements and holds.

Using the ASL word IDEA, the new analysis suggested that the word is formed by holding the hand in a certain handshape, location, orientation, and so forth; the hand is moved away from the body; finally, the hand is held in a different location. Thus, under this analysis, the word IDEA consists of two parameters—and the sequential pattern is Hold-Movement-Hold (HMH), as depicted in figure 6.

One final aspect of ASL words under this analysis completes the picture and brings it full circle in our comparison of signed and spoken words. Recall that spoken words are sequences of

Figure 6: Hold-Movement-Hold Analysis of IDEA

*Source:* Adapted by permission of the publisher, from C. Valli and C. Lucas, *Linguistics of American Sign Language: An Introduction*, 2d ed. (Washington, D.C.: Gallaudet University Press, 1995), 43.

phonemes /k/plus /æ/ plus /t/ for the word *cat.* These different sounds can be grouped in two major classes in spoken languages: consonants and vowels. In order to distinguish which consonant or which vowel is being produced, linguists use a system of *distinctive features* to describe how a sound is made. The vowel /æ/, for example, has a list of such features, usually represented as a set of binary (present or not-present) values. Taken together, features uniquely identify a particular phoneme. Importantly, these features are simultaneously associated with each phoneme.

The features for /æ/, for example, are simultaneously associated with /æ/. Thus, spoken languages exhibit both simultaneity (at the level of categorizing each individual sound) and sequentiality (at the level of combining sounds to form words).

As for signed words, under sequential analysis they, too, exhibit both simultaneity and sequentiality. The simultaneous element parallels the features of spoken languages: A limited set of features can be used to describe and uniquely identify the recombining parts of ASL words (Lane, Boyes-Braem, and Bellugi 1976; Johnson 1990). The parts, however, are combined in a sequential fashion to form signed words. Notice that there are many different movements and holds (the word IDEA, for example, has two different holds), but they can nevertheless be grouped into two major types.

This excursion into the structure of ASL words has examined only one level, which corresponds to the phonological study of spoken words described above. Indeed, as indicated by its title, this section has dealt with what ASL linguists commonly call ASL phonology. The phonology of spoken languages deals with how sounds are combined to form words. The phonology of signed languages deals with how gestures are combined to form words. These units are meaningless in themselves: /k/, /æ/, and /t/ have no meaning until they are combined to form /kæt/, *cat*. Likewise, the components of IDEA, the holds and movements of figure 6, do not on their own carry any meaning; only when they are combined to form IDEA does the unit as a whole acquire meaning.

In the next section, we will discuss combinations of meaningful units: morphemes. We will show that on this level especially, ASL differs radically from English.

## Another View of Words: ASL Morphology

As was explained in our discussion of ASL phonology, signed words, like spoken words, are made up of parts that can be recombined to form different words. There is another way in which spoken and signed words are made up of parts.

Recall that words are symbols. Words in spoken languages are not indivisible wholes. They can be broken down into smaller, meaningful parts called *morphemes*. A morpheme is the smallest combination of form and meaning. In the English word *cat* there is only one morpheme. *Cats*, however, has two morphemes: one morpheme is *cat*; the other morpheme is *-s*. Like *cat*, it has a form (/s/) and a meaning (more than one).

The way in which morphemes combine to form words varies across different languages. In chapter 1, we explained that many people believe ASL is a more "conceptual" language than English. We suggested that one reason for this may be that ASL packages concepts differently than English. What we called *packaging of concepts* is really one way to describe morphology. For the present discussion, the important distinction is the number of morphemes per word. There are languages, such as Chinese, in which words consist almost exclusively of single morphemes. These are called *isolating* languages. English, however, is a *synthetic* language. Such a language contains many more multi-morphemic words than does an isolating language.

Eskimo is an example of a third language category—*polysynthetic* language. A polysynthetic language contains an even greater number of multi-morphemic words than does a synthetic language; the difference is a matter of degree. There are greater possibilities of morpheme combinations in Eskimo than in English and Chinese. A verb in Eskimo can incorporate one or more nouns (e.g., the subject and the object). Like Eskimo, ASL is a polysynthetic language (Johnson and Liddell 1984).

Of course, not all words in ASL are multi-morphemic. Some words, such as LIKE, consist of single morphemes. By and large, however, one can combine many more morphemes into ASL words than into English words. What is more, the way that morphemes are combined in ASL is often quite different from the way they are combined in English.

Let us examine how three different languages combine morphemes to make words. Suppose a person wants to say, "I look at the girl for a long time." In English, of course, that is exactly how to say it. In German, the sentence might be, "Füreine Lange Zeit schaueich das Mädchenan." Translated *very* literally into English, this sentence means "For a long time look I the girl at." In Navajo, the sentence is the following:

| Asdzání | nish'ii- | go | níaagóó | nihoolzhiizo |
|---------|-----------------|-------|--------|-------------------------|
| woman | I-am-looking-at-her | while | far-to | time-markers-moved |

What about ASL? Let us look at the morphemic combinations and how they differ from those in English, German, and Navajo.

Before we compare these languages, however, we must make a diversion to explain how we will represent ASL in this text. For our discussion about ASL, we must rely on a written system for this signed language. Because there is currently no accepted form of written ASL, it is difficult to present an ASL sentence for discussion in a book. We did demonstrate a proposed writing system earlier, but to present sentences in that writing system would require readers to learn the system before they could understand our examples. Instead, we will rely on a commonly accepted written form; we will use glosses. Glosses are rough translations of ASL morphemes into English morphemes. The reader should understand, however, that the existence of glosses for ASL does not signify that ASL is English. The reader should also remember that glosses are not intended to be good translations into English of these ASL sentences. A good translation of the sentence has already been provided: "I look at the girl for a long time."

In ASL, the sentence will consist of just three words:

GIRL INDEX      I + LOOK-AT + HER + LONG-TIME
RIGHT

The first ASL word is one morpheme that indicates the object of the sentence. The second functions as an article: "the." The third word is more complex. It consists of the root word LOOK-AT, plus a morpheme to indicate the subject (first person singular), another morpheme to indicate the object (the girl), and yet another one to indicate that the activity of looking at the girl took place over an extended period of time.

The significant fact about these four examples is that although they all contain essentially the same information, they package this information differently.

There is another feature that ASL does not share with English: classifier morphology. Classifiers in ASL are combinations of two or more root morphemes (Padden 1987). One morpheme, the handshape, indicates the class of nouns to which the words belong, such as all people; upright objects, such as a boulder, a book, or a cup; surface vehicles, such as cars, bicycles, trucks, motorcycles, boats; round, thin objects, such as a coin or a cookie; long, thin objects, such as a pencil or pole; and many more. The second morpheme consists of a root movement that indicates the location and/or movement of the object. Examples are the following: a surface vehicle traveling up a long winding road, and several upright objects in a row on a long, flat object (perhaps a row of books on a bookshelf).

American Sign Language makes extensive use of classifier morphology not only in everyday conversations but also in ASL poetry and storytelling. It is in the area of classifiers that native English speakers often have the most difficulty in ASL. Classifiers are not used in the English language, and this may be why English structures interfere in the second language student's utterances in ASL. Fluency in the use and comprehension of classifiers is one mark of ASL competence. Because of this, activities using classifiers should be included at all levels of instruction.

*Putting Words into Sentences: ASL Syntax*

In any language, words must be combined in specific patterns to form sentences. For several years, people believed that ASL lacked any rigid sentence structure; indeed, it was once claimed that ASL did not even consist of sentences but merely of collections of signs. Researchers now know that, as do other languages, ASL has sentence-level grammar.

One way to examine the sentence structure of a language is to look at its basic word order. For example, the word order in English is essentially Subject-Verb-Object (SVO). This does not mean that sentences cannot be written in a different word order. People can say, for example, "The cake was eaten by the boy." The word order of this phrase is object, verb, subject.

The degree to which word order must be followed is influenced by several factors. One is the extent to which grammatical relations—who did what to whom—must be indicated by the order of words in a sentence. English, for example, relies on word order to indicate grammatical relations: "John loves Mary" is quite different from "Mary loves John." Other languages can make use of different devices to indicate grammatical relations. Often this is accomplished by means of the language's morphology: verbal affixes and case endings on nouns can indicate grammatical relations.

ASL is commonly considered an SVO word-order language. However, as was shown in the ASL example above, other orderings of words can be and are used. In the example, the girl was *topicalized.* Because she was the topic of interest, it was appropriate in ASL to move her to the front of the sentence. How does ASL indicate that *I* was looking at the *girl,* and not that *she* was looking at *me?*

In ASL, there are three classes of verbs (Padden 1987). One class uses ASL's morphology to incorporate the subject and object into the root verb. Examples of this class of verbs include GIVE, INFORM, ASK, SEND, HATE, and LOOK-AT. Verbs in this class change their form to indicate the person and number of the subject and object. For example, the ASL verb I-GIVE-YOU (first person singular subject and second person singular object) is different from the ASL verb YOU-GIVE-ME (second person singular subject and first person singular object) or HE/SHE/IT-GIVE-THEM (third person singular subject unmarked for gender and third person plural object also unmarked for gender). All three are obviously different from English because each word incorporates the verb, the subject, and the object. This is an excellent example of the polysynthetic nature of ASL.

A second class of ASL verbs does not contain morphology of the type described above. Words in this class include KNOW, LIKE, WALK, WANT, and FORGET. The form of the verb used in the sentence I LIKE YOU is the same as the form used in the sentence YOU LIKE ME. In sentences that use these verbs, the information for subject and object is contained in separate words for I and YOU. It is possible, however, for these words to be omitted in conversational signing. In response to the question, "Do you like coffee?", it is appropriate to respond, LIKE (with appropriate facial expression to indicate the degree—"I sort of like it," "I like it very much," and so forth)—omitting both the subject ("I") and the object ("coffee").

The final class of ASL verbs has already been mentioned: classifiers. Classifiers can incorporate verbs in ASL. Thus, a sentence such as "A car is traveling up a long and winding road" in ASL can contain just one word, the classifier VEHICLE, together with morphemes to indicate direction of motion, type of motion (straight, curved, zigzag, etc.), manner of motion (slow, fast, erratic, etc.), and more.

## It's Not All on the Hands

It would be a mistake for second language students of ASL to assume that all the information in ASL is contained on the hands. As shown earlier, the face is also used to transmit information. Facial expressions, body postures, and other nonmanual gestures are used to convey grammatical information. Generically, they are called *nonmanual signals* (NMSs).

Sometimes people compare NMSs in signed languages with voice qualities such as intonation or rhythm in spoken languages. The difference between NMSs and qualities such as intonation and rhythm is that NMSs are used to convey grammatical information in ASL. An example is the grammatical transformation of a statement into a question. Whereas the question in English, "Do you want to eat?", is typically produced with rising intonation, it is still a question whether this intonation is present or not. In English, the question is formed by rearranging the word order: "Do you want to eat?" versus "You do want to eat." In ASL, facial expressions mark different types of questions. For example, by adding a Yes/No facial marker, an ASL sentence consisting of four words, YOU MUST LEAVE YOU, becomes a question: "Do you have to leave?" Without the facial marker, it is no longer a question; it is a statement: "You have to leave."

NMSs are also used in ASL to indicate negatives ("You don't have to leave now"), relative clauses ("The boy who left is my son"), conditionals ("If you leave, I'll cry"), wh-questions

("Where do you have to go?"), and rhetorical questions ("I have to leave now. Why? Because I have another engagement across town.") where the addressee is not expected to answer the "Why?" question.

Nonmanual signals are also used in ASL to indicate adverbial information (Baker-Shenk and Cokely 1980c). For example, a characteristic facial expression usually written as *mm* is used in ASL sentences to mean "normally"; "regularly"; "going along fine"; "as expected." Another nonmanual signal, called *th*, indicates that a particular action was done in a careless or inattentive way. These adverbial nonmanual signals can be combined with ASL's verbal morphology in rich and complex ways. Take the English sentence, "I studied all night last night but didn't really pay much attention to what I was doing." In ASL this sentence would contain four words, LAST NIGHT I STUDY, with the verb STUDY containing all the richness that ASL's morphology makes possible to indicate the duration and manner of studying.

The nonmanual signal system in ASL is much more complex than has been conveyed in this short summary. Second language students of ASL must learn to use and understand this component of ASL if fluency is to be achieved.

## Manual Codes for English

Some readers might wonder why we include a discussion of English in a book about second language acquisition of ASL. Books on German, Spanish, or French do not generally discuss speaking or reading English. Why should a book about ASL contain a section on signing English?

Other readers might also note that manual codes for English are often held in low regard by many Deaf people. Why, they might ask, would we want to include a topic that is not a part of the culture of ASL users and that many Deaf people feel is an affront to the beauty and integrity of their language?

Many people believe that manual codes for English have done more damage than good to the lives of Deaf people. These people might ask why we would want to encourage, even indirectly, the continued use of these systems by teaching students about them. Finally, it is often claimed that exposing second language students to manual codes for English can impair their acquisition of ASL. At the very least, the argument goes, students should not be exposed to this English-based signing until their ASL competence has developed to the point where it will not be affected.

We believe that there are good reasons for early discussion of manual codes for English. It is true that manual codes for English are not ASL and should not be taught in an ASL course. Still, when adult students are first introduced to ASL they are uncertain about what it is. The myths that we discussed in chapter 1 are truly pervasive. Students who enter ASL courses are full of ideas about ASL and signed languages; many of these ideas, unfortunately, are incorrect and will prove to be detrimental to their acquisition of ASL. This is why we say that the early stages of instruction in ASL must involve a certain degree of *unlearning*.

German teachers may have to combat their students' uninformed ideas about the German language or German people. However, these teachers can be fairly confident that their students realize they are learning a different language. ASL students may not know that they are beginning on a journey toward learning another language. They may not understand that words in ASL are different from words in English. A common example of this is when a student asks the instructor, "How do you sign X [where X is some word in English] in ASL?" and expects one signed word in response.

We do understand and share many of Deaf people's feelings. We take issue, however, with the claim that manual codes for English are not a part of Deaf culture. They are certainly a part of Deaf people's experience. Deaf people know what manual codes for English look like. They have opinions about MCEs' effectiveness (or ineffectiveness) in education (see Bahan 1989c). Deaf people certainly have strong feelings about these systems. Experience, knowledge, opinions, feelings—this is culture. We want our students to know about these aspects of Deaf culture.

Thus, in answer to the third question, we would reply that the best way to ensure that manual codes for English are not mindlessly used by hearing people is not to ignore them, but to expose students to them. In part, this is merely a pragmatic decision. Students will gain access to information about manual codes for English whether we teach it or not, books containing vocabulary in manually coded English are readily available in most bookstores. We prefer that students' explorations, ponderings, and questions take place in the classroom. We are confident that thoughtful discussion among teachers and students about the relationship between spoken, signed, and written English and ASL—discussions that include Deaf people's attitudes towards manual codes for English, the history of hearing people's attempts to impose MCEs on Deaf people, and the documented evidence about their effectiveness in education—will enable students to arrive at their own informed conclusions.

Finally, there is no research showing that mere exposure to manual codes for English will have a negative effect on the second language learner's acquisition of ASL. Of course, any time spent in such discussions will be time taken from the central task of seeing and producing ASL. In the long run, however, it will be time well spent because it will make students more critically aware of what they are learning.

It may also be that, depending on the teacher's or the program's philosophy, such discussions will not be possible in an ASL class. In some programs, for example, English is never allowed under any circumstances in an ASL classroom. Thus, in the early stages of learning, when students most need to discuss theoretical and cultural information, they are the least able to undertake such a discussion in ASL. In these circumstances, a program may require students to take an introductory course in which ASL cultural issues and myths about signed languages are examined. In programs that do not offer such a course, perhaps special days can be set aside for discussion about attitudes and myths—topics that are vital to the students' continued development, but for which they do not yet possess sufficiently advanced fluency for conversation in ASL.

At the beginning of this chapter, it was said that English is a language that can be represented in all three of the major modalities: spoken, written, and signed. What does it mean to say that one can sign English? What are manual codes for English? In order to understand this question, readers must first explore what it means to say one can write English.

The creation of a writing system can be understood as a design problem with two design questions: What will the written symbols represent, and how will the symbols be invented?

Writing can represent units at the primary or at the secondary level of language. At one level, written marks (usually called graphs) can represent meaningful units either single morphemes or polymorphemic units, such as words, phrases, or sentences. These types of writing systems are called *logographic* (see figure 7). By far the most common are systems that write morphemes. Written Chinese is a logographic system. The graphs of Chinese

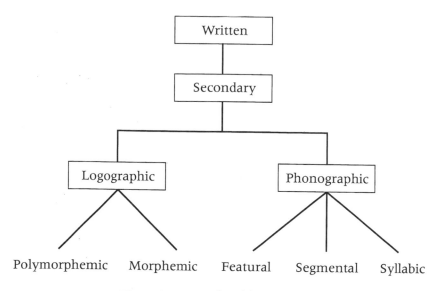

Figure 7: Types of Writing Systems

represent morphemes (although, as explained earlier, for the most part Chinese words are monomorphemic, so we may just as well say that Chinese writes words).

Writing systems also can represent units at the other level of language. Graphs can represent the nonmeaningful level of sounds. Such writing systems are called *phonographic.* At least three solutions to phonographic writing are possible: writing features, writing segments (consonants and vowels), or writing syllables. Written English is an example of *segmental* writing. These types of writing systems are often given the generic name *alphabetic* writing.

The second design question concerns the source of the marks used in the writing system—the script. Two general solutions to this design question exist: invent a new script, or borrow and adapt an existing script. By far the most common solution is to borrow and modify existing scripts. For example, written English came from the ancient Phoenician script, through Semitic, Greek, and Roman writing systems.

Like written English, manual codes for English are secondary representations of English in another modality. The same two design questions that must be asked for devising a writing system must also be asked for devising a manual code for English: What language feature will be represented (words, syllables, sounds, or some combination of these), and where will we get the signed "marks"?

Because manual codes for English systems are invented, there is no one solution to the design questions posed. There are, however, two common themes that run through many of the more popular systems. One is that MCE systems typically are logographic. That is one manually coded unit (a sign, comparable to a graph) represents a morpheme of English. Thus, in one MCE system, the sentence "He established those policies yesterday" would be expressed using eight signs: HE ESTABLISH PAST-TENSE THOSE POLICY PLURAL YESTER DAY.

The second theme concerns the source for the signs in MCE systems. As is true for writing systems, the most common solution is to borrow. Épée borrowed from Old French Sign Language when he and others devised French methodical signs. Modern manual codes for English were also devised with borrowed signs. In most of the MCE systems, the source for signs is the lexical stock of ASL.

The complete analysis of manual codes for English is far more complex than is portrayed here. Most of these systems attempt not merely to represent spoken English, but also to represent in some way the complex relationship between spoken and written English.

There is a popular tendency these days to claim that manual codes for English are not languages. Usually, what is meant is that manual codes for English do not seem to be viable substitutes for primary languages, such as spoken English or signed ASL (see, for example, Supalla 1986). Manual codes for English are ineffective as primary languages. We must point out, however, that just as written English is English, written Chinese is Chinese, and written Korean is Korean, so manual codes for English are English. To dismiss MCE systems as "not language" makes no more sense than it would to dismiss writing systems as "not language." The evaluation of the effectiveness of such systems, both as pedagogical tools and as effective systems for representing primary language, is a matter that is beyond the scope of this book.

## The Multilingual Nature of the Deaf Community

From all that has been said thus far, it should be clear that the Deaf community is linguistically complex. At least two languages, ASL and English, are used in the community. A third language is also common Pidgin Sign English (to be discussed in the succeeding pages). In addition, the Deaf community is tri-modal; that is, all three modes—speaking, writing, and signing—are present.

In order to function in the Deaf community, members must know how and when to use these three languages and modalities. Second language students of ASL must share at least some of this knowledge if they are to communicate effectively with Deaf people.

## Bilingualism

The Deaf community is a bilingual society. In order to explain how this is so, we define two types of bilingualism: societal bilingualism and individual bilingualism.

In societal bilingualism, two or more languages are used in the everyday life of a community. Societal bilingualism can be the result of the movement of people because of political, economic, cultural, or religious reasons (Grosjean 1982). Usually, when two groups, who do not share the same language, come into contact, one takes a majority and the other a minority position. This situation occurs in many of the world's colonized countries. In such a circumstance, it is not unusual to see the minority group learn the majority group's language, either for pragmatic reasons (they must learn to get along with the majority) or because the majority language has been forced on the minority. In the latter case, it is also not unusual for the majority to actively suppress the minority's language.

One good place to examine the status of a minority language is in the field of education. In many cases of societal bilingualism, the majority language is the only one used in school. The minority student must learn by means of this language. With few exceptions, this is the case for deaf students in this country. ASL is not an accepted language of instruction in residential schools, in mainstream programs, or in postsecondary education. Until recently, not even Gallaudet University, the world's only liberal arts university for deaf students, supported the use of ASL in the classroom.

Societal bilingualism evolves over time (Grosjean 1987). A society can either retain its bilingualism or shift to monolingualism. Often, this has little to do with whether the minority language is accorded recognition in the majority community's political or educational institutions. For example, although ASL has been poorly understood by hearing people and still plays a minor role in deaf education, there is no evidence that ASL is a dying language or that the Deaf community is shifting to English monolingualism (Nash 1987).

It is not the case that each individual in a bilingual society is bilingual. In a bilingual society such as Canada, for instance, some individuals are bilingual, whereas others may be monolingual in either English or French. Important issues in the study of individual bilingualism include how an individual acquired his or her two languages; in which situations they were acquired; how bilinguals separate the two languages in their cognitive system; how bilinguals interact with monolinguals and other bilinguals; and the effects of bilingualism on personality and cognitive development.

In some cases, an individual bilingual may have learned one language in the home and another at school. This is frequently the case with Spanish speakers in the Southwest. Bilinguals often keep their two languages totally separate. One language will be used for conversing with certain people in particular settings, the other language will be used for talking with other people or in other settings. On the other hand, bilinguals sometimes combine their languages when they are talking with someone who knows both languages. This process is called *code-switching*. Code-switching is a rule-governed way of using two languages; it is not the mere haphazard mixing of two languages (Gumperz and Hernandez-Chavez 1971). Code-switching should not be taken as evidence that bilinguals are confused about when or how to use their two languages. In particular, code-switching among bilingual children should not be misunderstood to mean that the children are *language confused*. For example, there are Deaf children who know and use ASL (which they have learned from Deaf adults or from peers) and English (which they have learned from their teachers). These children will often code-switch between the two languages. This is a natural developmental pattern for many deaf children (Wilcox and Corwin 1990).

Although most Deaf people are bilingual to some extent, there is variation among individuals (Kannapell 1989). Some Deaf people are fully bilingual in ASL and English. Many Deaf people have been raised in Deaf families where ASL was their first language. That they have gone on to attain Ph.D. degrees in fields such as psychology, education, or linguistics clearly indicates that they are also fluent in English. Other Deaf people may be fluent in ASL but have only marginal English language skills. (Generally, this is taken to mean reading and writing rather than speaking skills.) Other Deaf people, who were born into hearing families where English was their native language, have gone on to learn ASL and become enculturated into the Deaf community.

## Sociolinguistic Variation

Second language students should know that although Deaf people across the United States use ASL, variation in ASL does occur (Valli 1992). One way to understand the nature of this variation is to recall the various levels of linguistic structure: phonological (pronunciation), lexical (words), and syntactic (sentences). Variation can occur at any of these levels. This variation is called sociolinguistic when it is related to a social factor. Typical social factors that affect sociolinguistic variation are age, geography, sex, education, and race.

Woodward (1980) described many types of sociolinguistic variation in ASL. For example, there exists a dialect of Black Southern signing used by Black Deaf people in the southeastern United States. Other common types of sociolinguistic variation in ASL are regional (geographic) variation, social (education) variation, gender variation, and age variation.

## Pidgin Sign English

Whenever two languages come into contact, it is common to see a special variety of language appear, called a pidgin. Pidgins develop from the need of the two language communities to communicate with each other. Pidgins are characterized by a mixture of structures from the two languages, by the appearance of structures that are not present in either of the two contact languages, and by a reduction in structure in comparison with the contact languages. Pidgins are, by definition, not one's native language. They are often used in restricted social settings and frequently have negative attitudes attached to their use.

Woodward (1980) has suggested that a pidgin language developed out of the contact between ASL and English. This language is called Pidgin Sign English (PSE). There is not one monolithic variety of PSE. Variation in PSE occurs in a rule-governed way. The variation correlates with such social variables as whether the signer is deaf or hearing, has deaf or hearing parents, learned to sign before or after the age of six, and attended some or no college (Woodward 1973).

Cokely (1983) proposed that PSE could be analyzed not as a pidgin but as foreigner talk and learner's grammar. This description places less emphasis on PSE as a language; instead, it describes this type of signing as reflecting the accommodations that Deaf people make when communicating with less fluent, hearing ASL users. Of course, at some level, the processes of accommodation that take place in foreigner talk must be similar to those that take place in language contact situations that lead to the development of pidgins. Also, the analysis of PSE as foreigner talk does not explain a phenomenon that is a common experience for many second language students. Frequently, when Deaf people find out that the person with whom they have been using ASL is hearing, they switch to a form of PSE (Kannapell 1989). Clearly, this cannot be the result of a conscious or unconscious effort to facilitate communication. Before the Deaf person realized that the other person was hearing, communication in ASL was proceeding without any problems. A more reasonable explanation is that ASL functions to maintain the Deaf community's identity. Switching to a form of PSE is a way of reestablishing the cultural boundaries that were violated by a hearing person using ASL (Kannapell 1989).

Whatever linguists ultimately decide about how PSE should be classified, it is important for second language students to be aware of this variety of signed language because it is so pervasive in Deaf/hearing interactions.

*Language Attitudes*

The preceding description should make it clear that there are specific and strong attitudes associated with languages in the Deaf community. It is important for second language learners to be exposed to these attitudes for two reasons. First, it will help them to understand Deaf people and the cultural context in which ASL is situated. Second, some of the strong attitudes that Deaf people have are directed at hearing people who use ASL.

Deaf people are often ambivalent in their attitudes toward ASL and English (Kannapell 1987). ASL is the language with which they identify. It is the language that sets Deaf people apart as a people and that embodies the deaf experience. At the same time they recognize that ASL is little valued in American society and that in order to get ahead in education or employment they need to be proficient in English.

ASL functions not only to create a bond of identity among its users; it also functions to keep outsiders out. Deaf people often look with suspicion at hearing people who are learning ASL as a second language. As noted above, Deaf people will often switch to an English form of signing when they interact with hearing people. This is as much an attempt to maintain the integrity of the group as it is the fact that in most cases hearing people are not fluent users of ASL.

The use of ASL to maintain cultural boundaries is directed not only toward hearing people. Deaf ASL users will also avoid or exclude deaf people who use English-like signing such as PSE or MCE. Classification of people according to their language preference is an important way that Deaf culture enables Deaf people to perceive and understand their world.

## ASL as a Foreign Language

Two movements have begun to spread across the United States in the past several years. One is the rapidly increasing enrollment in ASL classes. The second is the tremendous interest

Table 2. Comparison of ASL Course Enrollment, 1986 and 1991

| Program Type | 1986 | 1991 | Growth |
|---|---|---|---|
| Community colleges and technical schools | 1098 | 1529 | 139% |
| Colleges and universities | 935 | 2111 | 226% |
| All programs | 2263 | 4094 | 181% |

*Note:* The data were collected from ASL Program Directors in 1991.

in acceptance of ASL in fulfillment of foreign language require-ments in high schools, colleges, and universities.

## Growth in ASL Instruction

"The movement to accept ASL throughout America is like a slow building groundswell of water," according to Gary W. Olsen, former Executive Director of the National Association of the Deaf. "It gains momentum as it swells and so does the accep-tance of ASL" (Olsen 1988, 107). The magnitude of this momen-tum is hinted at in the results of a survey of ASL instruction conducted in the early 1990s. The survey was mailed to ASL in-structional programs in colleges, universities, technical schools, community colleges, and private and public service agencies across the country. Table 2 lists 1986 enrollment and the percent-age of growth for all 43 programs reporting. Table 2 also includes figures for two categories of respondents: colleges and universi-ties, and community colleges and technical schools.

In the programs reported, hearing and deaf instructors were equally represented. The majority of the instructors held degrees at the master's level (44%), with 33 percent holding bachelor's level degrees, 9 percent holding associate level degrees, 6 percent holding doctoral degrees, and 8 percent with no degree beyond a high school diploma.

The overwhelming majority of programs surveyed (98%) re-ported that Deaf culture was taught in their ASL courses. Only 35 percent of the programs, however, reported that they offered a separate course in Deaf culture for those students who wanted more knowledge of the way of life of Deaf people.

The most popular ASL books used by the programs that responded were *A Basic Course in American Sign Language* (Humphries, Padden, and O'Rourke 1980), *American Sign Language* (Baker-Shenk and Cokely 1980a), and the Vista College *Signing Naturally* series.

One commonly asked question is whether ASL is really being taught in such programs. It is difficult to determine this from responses to a survey, but a tentative conclusion can be drawn based on the overall results. At least half of the courses are being taught by Deaf people. Fifty percent of the instructors have at least a master's degree. The materials most commonly used are among the best available for teaching ASL. It seems that this young profession is doing remarkably well.

One unexpected finding from the survey was the number of high schools across the country that offer ASL to hearing students. As more states mandate the acceptance of ASL in fulfillment of high school foreign language requirements, this trend will continue. Little is known about who is teaching high school ASL courses, about whether they are actually teaching ASL (and not PSE or MCE), nor about the long-term impact on college-level programs. A survey of high schools would probably result in valuable information about the current growth of ASL in America.

### Acceptance of ASL as a Foreign Language

Until recently, the groundswell of interest in ASL had made little impact on foreign language policy in schools. Although ASL has a long and rich history in America and scholarly research on ASL is in its fourth decade, ASL has been slow to garner any degree of status as an acceptable alternative to fulfill foreign language requirements. This, too, is beginning to change. Acceptance of ASL as a foreign language is now a topic of debate at many American colleges and universities and in many of our state legislatures.

Determining exactly which schools accept ASL as a foreign language is a difficult undertaking. There are several factors to consider, and they intermingle to form the following major types of cases:

- Schools that do not have foreign language requirements, and therefore do not have policies for accepting (or rejecting) ASL as a foreign language, even though they may teach ASL.
- Schools that do not have foreign language requirements but nevertheless have considered the matter of ASL and have come out in support of ASL as a foreign language.
- Schools that have foreign language requirements but have never considered the possibility of accepting ASL in fulfillment of the requirement.
- Schools that have foreign language requirements and have allowed certain individuals to fulfill the requirement with ASL on an *ad hoc* basis.
- Schools that have foreign language requirements and have formal policies allowing certain groups of students, for example deaf students or students majoring in deaf education, to fulfill the requirement with ASL.
- Schools that have foreign language requirements and have formal policies allowing any student to fulfill the requirement with ASL.

Often more than one of these situations will be represented within the same school. It is possible, for example, for the college of arts and sciences at a large university to have a formal policy accepting ASL in fulfillment of a foreign language requirement, whereas the college of engineering or education at the same university has no such policy and may even have decided not to accept ASL in fulfillment of its requirements.

Clearly, of the six situations listed the most important in the movement to accept ASL as a foreign language is the last: schools with formal policies accepting ASL as a foreign language. Schools that fall into this category include: California State University (all campuses); Garner Webb University, North Carolina; Madonna College, Michigan; Michigan State University; Northeastern University, Boston; State University of New York at Stony Brook; University of Arkansas; University of Arizona; University of New Hampshire at Manchester; University of New Mexico; University of Minnesota; University of Rochester, New York; University of South Florida; University of Washington; William Rainey Harper College, Illinois. (See appendix 4 for an expanded list of universities and colleges that accept ASL as partial or complete fulfillment of foreign language requirements.)

Activity is also taking place in state legislatures to recognize and accept ASL as a foreign language. In fact, legal precedent has been established for this recognition within the framework of federal and state laws in more than 25 states, including Alaska, California, Connecticut, Florida, Illinois, Maine, Michigan, Pennsylvania, Texas, Utah, and Washington, all of which recognize ASL as a foreign language for the purpose of meeting high school graduation requirements (Forestal forthcoming).

Finally, the recognition and acceptance of natural signed languages has become international in scope. In 1988, the parliament of the European Community, noting that there are 500,000 profoundly deaf people in Member States whose first language is their national signed language and not the dominant mother tongue of their country, recognized as legitimate languages the indigenous signed languages of the twelve Member States. Recognition and acceptance of signed languages is clearly an idea whose time has come.

## Notes

1. Old French Sign Language is also commonly known as *langue des signes français (LSF)*.

2. In many parts of the country, especially the East and West coasts, the ASL word CHINESE is decreasing in usage. Recent interactions with Chinese Deaf people have led to the widespread adoption of what is erroneously considered to be the Chinese Sign Language (CSL) word for CHINA. Actually, in CSL, the sign means "Beijing."

# 3

# American Deaf Culture

It is common for the general public to consider deaf people in this country as handicapped Americans with no further sense of identity as a people. This is far from correct. There exists a strong and tightknit group of people in the United States that identifies itself with Deaf culture (Wilcox 1989). As with any culture, its members share values, beliefs, attitudes, and, most importantly, a language different from that of outsiders to the culture.

Of course, like Hispanics, Jews, Navajos, or any other cultural group in the United States, Deaf people do not consider themselves "foreigners." The Navajo code-talkers, who became famous during World War II when they were used to communicate secret information in Navajo via radio, would surely resist any attempt to be called non-American. They would just as surely resent any characterization that did not recognize their Navajo cultural heritage.

This is not to say that all deaf people in America are members of Deaf culture merely because they cannot hear. Entry into a culture is never merely a matter of being born Hispanic, Jewish, Navajo, Black, deaf, and so forth. Cultural values are shared; members must learn, accept, and share the values of the group before they can be said to be a part of that culture. The same is true for Deaf culture.

Although the term *Deaf culture* is used frequently, it is not meant to imply that Deaf people the world over share the same culture. Deaf Americans are members of American Deaf culture; British Deaf people are members of British Deaf culture. British Deaf people and American Deaf people use two different languages, share different experiences, and have different historical backgrounds. Still, there are some values that British and American Deaf people share merely because they are united by at least one common experience: They are Deaf people living in a society in which hearing people dominate. This singular bond of common experience is known to other cultural groups as well. German Jews and American Jews, for example, do not share the same culture. Yet, because of a common experience—their Jewish religion and heritage—Jewish people the world over do share some core of commonality.

If being deaf (having a hearing loss) is not sufficient to qualify a person as a member of the Deaf culture, how does one gain entry into Deaf culture? To rephrase this question: Who are Deaf people? In order to understand this question and to find a cultural answer to it, let us first discuss what is meant by culture.

## Culture: Looking at the World from the Native's Point of View

Perhaps it is best to start by explaining what is not meant by culture. Culture is commonly thought to consist of things, the material objects that people possess and use. Although books, boats, clothes, and houses can tell us about the culture of a group of people, they are not the culture. Anthropologists call these objects *artifacts.*

Culture is not a laundry list of traits and facts about a group of people. It is not the higher class status one achieves by attending opera performances, reading the Greek classics, going to an art museum, or learning aristocratic manners. Culture is not something that can be bought, sold, or handed out. Culture is also not the romantic heritage of a group of people as seen through their music, dance, holidays, religion, and so forth, although culture may be reflected in them.

Finally, culture should not be confused with biological traits such as race. The reason Jews, Blacks, Hispanics, or Navajos share a culture is not because they are born Jewish, Black, Hispanic, or Navajo. Consider the following hypothetical situation. Suppose a young Navajo boy is born to a Navajo couple. When the child is six months old, the mother and father are killed in an automobile accident. The child is adopted by a young Anglo family; the father is an accountant and the mother is a pediatrician. Before the child's first birthday, the family moves to downtown Manhattan. The boy attends private schools in Manhattan and, when he graduates from high school, receives a scholarship from New York University. He attends that university for two years, majoring in computer engineering.

We now ask: Is this young man Navajo? In one sense, he is—his genetic heritage is certainly Navajo. He will look like a Navajo. But in another sense, he definitely is not Navajo. He does not share any experiences with other Navajos. He does not share their language and does not know how Navajos behave. He will not act like a Navajo. Racially, the young man is a Navajo; culturally, he is not. What, then, is culture? Anthropologist Ward Goodenough (1957) writes the following definition:

> Culture consists of whatever it is one has to know or believe in order to operate in a manner acceptable to its members. . . . It is the forms of things that people have in mind, their models for perceiving, relating, and otherwise interpreting them. (p. 167)

Culture is how one makes sense of the world. It is the ideas, concepts, categories, values, beliefs—what Clifford Geertz calls the "machinery" that people use "to orient themselves in a world otherwise opaque" (Geertz 1973, 363). The study of culture consists of learning about how a group of people makes sense of the world. Geertz (1983, 55) writes that the study of culture requires that one sees "things from the native's point of view." This does not mean an individual must "become one" with another, but merely put a particular perspective aside for the moment and try to learn what the world looks like to others.

> The trick is not to get yourself into some inner correspondence of spirit with your informants. Preferring, like the rest of us, to call their souls their own, they are not going to be altogether keen about such an effort anyhow. The trick is to figure out what the devil they think they are up to. (Geertz 1983, p. 58)

One of the things that people are up to is figuring out who populates their world. Culture helps us to categorize people. Again, Geertz (1973) illuminates how this works.

> Peoples everywhere have developed symbolic structures in terms of which persons are perceived not baldly as such, as mere unadorned members of the human race, but as representatives of certain distinct categories of persons, specific sorts of individuals. . . . The everyday world in which the members of any community move, their taken-for-granted field of social action, is populated not by anybodies, faceless men without qualities, but by somebodies, concrete classes of determinate persons positively characterized and appropriately labeled. (p. 363)

The first task in the study of Deaf culture is to figure out who Deaf people think they are. From the Deaf person's point of view, who qualifies as a Deaf person and who does not? What are the "distinct categories of persons" that Deaf culture imposes on the world? If the world as seen through Deaf eyes is not populated by faceless people without qualities, who are the somebodies who are positively characterized and appropriately labeled?

Rather than answer these questions directly, we would like instead to demonstrate an approach that allows students to discover the answers themselves. It is possible to figure out who people think they are by looking at who they think other people are. People can learn much about themselves by looking at their "polar opposites." Judy Grahn (1984) explains this concept:

> The groups often considered "polar opposites" in our culture— men and women, Gays and straights, Blacks and whites—serve as

mirrors for each other, giving each of us vital information concerning our roles in society. Without mirrors, how well would any of us know ourselves? (p. 51)

Let us turn this around. By examining what a group thinks about "us"—their opposites—we can learn a great deal about who they think "they" are.

*Portraits of the Whiteman*

To demonstrate, we will use an example described by Keith Basso (1979) in a book entitled *Portraits of "the Whiteman": Linguistic Play and Cultural Symbols Among the Western Apache.* While working with the Western Apache Indians in Arizona, Basso noted that they often enjoyed sharing joking characterizations of White people. The following scene is an example (Basso 1979, 46–47).

> [At the home of J. His wife, K, is washing the dishes. J is talking to K. He starts to say something but is interrupted by a knock on the door. He rises, answers the knock, and finds L standing outside.]
>
> J: Hello my friend! How you doing? How you feeling, L? You feeling good?
>
> [J now turns in the direction of K and addresses her.]
>
> J: Look who here, everybody! Look who just come in. Sure, it's my good Indian friend, L. Pretty good all right!
>
> [J slaps L on the shoulder and, looking him directly in the eyes, seizes his hand and pumps it wildly up and down.]
>
> J: Come right in, friend! Don't stay outside in the rain. Better you come in right now.
>
> [J now drapes his arm around L's shoulder and moves him in the direction of a chair.]
>
> J: Sit down! Sit right down! Take you loads off you ass. You hungry? You want some beer? Maybe you want some wine? You want crackers? Bread? You want some sandwich? How 'bout it? You hungry? I don't know. Maybe you get sick. Maybe you don't eat again long time.
>
> [K has stopped washing dishes and is looking on with amusement. L has seated himself and has a look of bemused resignation on his face.]

J:  You sure looking good to me, L. You looking pretty fat! Pretty
good all right! You got new boots? Where you buy them? Sure
pretty good boots! I glad . . .

[At this point J breaks into laughter. K joins in. L shakes his head
and smiles. The joke is over.]

K:  indaa' dogoyááda! ("Whitemen are stupid!")

The reader at this point probably wonders what was so funny
about all of this—why are Whitemen so stupid? Basso explains by
showing how the Apache have taken White people's behavior, in
this case their ways of talking, and used them to make fun of
White people.

1. **Hello my friend!** Indians think that White people throw
around the term *friend* in an irresponsible way. There is no word
in Apache that corresponds to friend; the closest they have is a
phrase used for people they have known many years and for
whom they have developed a strong sense of confidence and
respect.

2. **How you doing? How you feeling?** Except among persons who enjoy quite close relations, unsolicited queries about
an individual's health or emotional state constitute impertinent
violations of personal privacy.

3. **Look who here everybody!** When an Apache joins or
departs from a social gathering, he or she prefers to go about it un-
obtrusively.

4. **Personal name.** In Apache culture, personal names are
considered to be items of individually owned property. Calling
someone by name is sometimes likened to temporarily borrowing
a valued possession.

5. **J slaps L on the back, shakes his hand, looks him directly in the eye, and guides him to a chair.** Except when
participating in physical activities that require contact, Apaches
are careful to avoid touching. This is especially true of adult men.
Backslapping and handshaking are considered a direct encroach-
ment on a person's private territory; if it lingers without apparent
reason, it provides grounds for suspicion because of its homosex-
ual overtones. Prolonged eye contact is interpreted as an act of

aggression. Steering a person to a chair would be considered an outright violation of a person's freedom of movement.

6. **Come right in, my friend! Don't stay outside in the rain. Sit down!** Utterances in the imperative mode are considered bossing someone around and quite offensive. If a visitor wants to enter a home and sit down, he will ask permission. It is considered just as polite to take care of business at the door. If an Apache wants to issue a directive, he will do so in an oblique way. For example, if he wants to say, "Don't go hunting without a jacket" he would possibly say, "There are lots of mosquitos today."

7. **You hungry? You want some beer . . . wine . . . crackers . . . bread . . . How 'bout it . . . You hungry?** Apaches consider it rude to repeat a question several times. It is also considered discourteous to demand replies before a person is ready. Asking the same question, rapidly, is interpreted as anger or irritation.

8. **I don't know. Maybe you get sick.** Apaches hold firmly to the belief that talking about trouble and adversity can increase the chances of its occurrence.

9. **You sure looking good to me, L. You got new boots?** Remarks concerning a person's physical appearance are not polite, because they focus attention on aspects of one's private person.

One can now see what is wrong with the way White people talk from the Apache perspective, everything is wrong! Everything that a White person says, his entire demeanor seems to be rude, inconsiderate, or offensive. No wonder Apaches believe White people are stupid.

Of course, White people do not feel that they are being rude, inconsiderate, or offensive. In fact, not to act in the way they do—to avoid looking at a person, not to offer food, or to fail to attend to a person's personal appearance—may be considered just as offensive to some White people. The Apaches' characterizations of White people are not portraits of how White people really are. They are culturally conceived portraits, cultural constructions. As Basso (1979, 4) describes it, "'The Whiteman' is a model of Whitemen—who Whitemen are, how they contrast with other forms of humanity, and what they stand for." As a cultural construction, a model invented by Apaches, "The Whiteman" actually tells us more about the Apache view of the world than it tells us about how white people view the world. It is a mirror of Apache culture. By saying who they think White people are, Apaches say more about who they think they themselves are.

### A Portrait of the Hearing Person

Let us use the above example to approach the study of Deaf culture. The goal is to see the world from the Deaf person's point of view. Hearing people can begin to examine Deaf culture by trying to understand how Deaf people view hearing people. Students could begin by using the Deaf equivalent of a "Portrait of the Whiteman"—a "Portrait of the Hearing Person."

Such a portrait is to be found in a play first performed in 1973 by the National Theatre of the Deaf entitled "My Third Eye." In one part of the play, a group of Deaf actors are shown performing in a sideshow. The feeling is almost as if they had recently returned from an expedition into a strange land—the Land of the Hearing—and are now sharing with their comrades what they saw. Several of the actors are standing around. One woman is dressed as the sideshow ringmaster. To the side is a cage with people inside—they are hearing people. The ringmaster steps forward.

> RM:  Here is the exhibit. See yourselves! Body shape the same. Limbs the same. Behavior—*ah, different!* You and I use our eyes.
>
> [The other actors demonstrate various uses of their eyes to communicate.]
>
> RM:  Hers are blank, weak. You and I use our faces.
>
> [Again, the actors demonstrate various uses of their faces to communicate.]
>
> RM:  Hers is frozen except around the mouth. You will notice that the mouths continue to move throughout this performance.
>
> RM:  Let our actors show you what we saw.
>
> [A woman is shown talking on the phone. Although we can see her mouth move, we cannot hear her voice.]

RM:  See what happens? Nothing can stop her!

[The actors come up one by one and try to get her attention by talking to her and pulling at her arm.

Eventually, one strong young man picks her up and turns her completely upside down; nonplussed, she continues to talk on the phone.]

RM:  In that world, we saw that because they do not use their hands, they have a fear of touching.

[The actors are shown as hearing people on a subway. The car is full of people standing, holding on to the overhead rails. One man enters and tries to move his way forward through the people. As he does so, he clearly is afraid of touching people to get their attention. When he does overcome his fear and taps a woman passenger on the shoulder, she is startled and jumps back in terror.]

What does the hearing person learn from this portrait of hearing people? What becomes obvious is that the behavior of hearing people seems quite strange to Deaf people. From the Deaf perspective, hearing people do not use their eyes and faces to communicate. Because of this, our Deaf "anthropologists" speculate that hearing people's eyes are weak and their faces frozen. Instead of communicating in a "normal" fashion, hearing people move their mouths. What is more, nothing seems to be coming out of their mouths—they merely continue to move. Instead of communicating in a face-to-face manner with live people, they seem to derive odd pleasure out of moving their mouths for long periods of time in front of strange pieces of machinery. Finally, Deaf people speculate that hearing people have a fear of touching. The Deaf ringmaster offers a reasonable explanation for this (reasonable, that is, from the ringmaster's perspective): It is because the hearing do not use their hands to communicate.

How accurate is the Deaf portrait of hearing people? Hearing people may feel that it is inaccurate: They may feel that their eyes are not weak nor their faces frozen. They use their eyes and faces in perfectly appropriate ways (appropriate, that is, for hearing people). They probably do not feel that they are afraid to touch. Rather, they feel that they know exactly when and how much to touch.

This portrait of the hearing person, like Basso's portrait, reveals more about the people painting the portrait than it does about the people portrayed. It reveals that Deaf people value their eyes. They value the use of the face to convey information. Excessive movement of the mouth, on the other hand, may be an unacceptable behavior in Deaf culture. Finally, Deaf people value touching.

## Becoming Enculturated into the Deaf World

One may suppose that for Deaf people, as for all people, there exist at least two major types of people: "us" and "them." Children start life assuming that everyone is the same. Cultures teach them to differentiate: *Some people are like us, but most of the world is different.* The child's task, in becoming enculturated, is to figure out who "we" are and who "they" are.

For the Deaf child, the task is no different. In their wonderful book on Deaf culture, *Deaf in America: Voices from a Culture,* Carol Padden and Tom Humphries (1988) relate a story about a child acquiring this sense of "us" and "them." They tell about Sam Supalla, who is now a Deaf educator and professor at the University of Arizona. Sam was born into a Deaf family with several Deaf older brothers.

As his interests turned to the world outside his family, he noticed a girl next door who seemed to be about his age. After a few tentative encounters, they became friends. She was a satisfactory playmate, but there was a problem of her "strangeness." He could not talk with her as he could with his older brothers and his parents. She seemed to have extreme difficulty understanding even the crudest gestures. After a few futile attempts to converse, he gave up and instead pointed when he wanted to go somewhere. He wondered what strange affliction his friend had, but since they had developed a way to interact with each other, he was content to accommodate to her peculiar needs. One day, Sam remembers vividly, he finally understood that his friend was indeed odd. They were playing in her home, when suddenly her mother walked up to them and animatedly began to move her mouth. As if by magic, the girl picked up a dollhouse and moved it to another place. Sam was mystified and went home to ask his mother about exactly what kind of affliction the girl next door had. His mother explained that she was HEARING and because of this did not know how to SIGN; instead she and her mother TALK, they move their mouths to communicate with each other. Sam then asked if this girl and her family were the only ones "like that." His mother explained that no, in fact, nearly everyone else was like the neighbors. It was his own family that was unusual. It was a memorable moment for Sam. He remembers thinking how curious the girl next door was, and if she was HEARING, how curious HEARING people were. (pp. 15–16)

As Deaf children such as Sam become Deaf adults, they learn Deaf cultural values from other members of the community. Many people other than those we have mentioned here populate the Deaf world. In addition to DEAF[1] and HEARING people, there are HARD OF HEARING people—those who straddle a fine line between the Deaf and the hearing worlds. There are also ORAL people who, in the perception of Deaf people, embrace the hearing world and reject their identity as Deaf people. Finally, there are THINK-HEARING people—a strongly pejorative ASL term (not unlike "Uncle Tom") for deaf people who accept uncritically the ideology of the hearing world (Padden and Humphries 1988).

## A Model of Deaf Culture

In their book on ASL instruction (1980b), Charlotte Baker-Shenk and Dennis Cokely proposed a model of Deaf culture that is useful for summarizing the values and characteristics introduced earlier. The model is depicted in figure 8.

The model proposes four essential factors involved in defining members of Deaf culture. One is audiological; in order to be a member of Deaf culture one must have a hearing loss. The degree of hearing loss is not as critical as one might expect. It is quite possible for a person who is perceived as a culturally Deaf person to have much less of a hearing loss than another deaf person who may be perceived as ORAL or THINK-HEARING.

Another factor is social: There is significance in the degree to which a person associates with Deaf people, perhaps by attending a school for the deaf, marrying a Deaf person, going to the Deaf Club or Deaf community events, and so forth. The third factor is political—the extent to which the person wields power in Deaf community affairs. An example of how one acquires power in the Deaf community would be serving as an officer in a Deaf organization.

Finally, the fourth, and one of the most important, factor in determining who is a member of Deaf culture is linguistic—the extent to which the individual uses and supports the use of ASL. ASL is a central feature of Deaf culture. It is the glue that holds

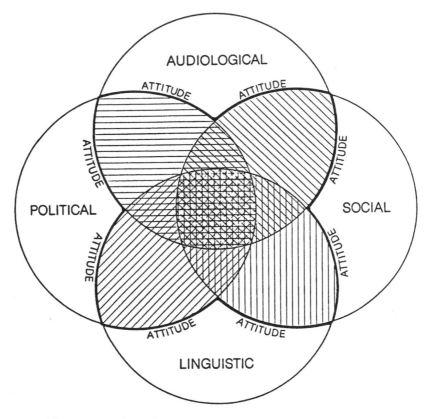

Figure 8:  Baker-Shenk and Cokely Model of Deaf Culture

*Source:* Reprinted, by permission of the publisher, from C. Baker-Shenk and D. Cokely, *American Sign Language: A Teacher's Resource Text on Curriculum, Methods, and Evaluation* (Washington, D.C.: Gallaudet University Press, 1980), 18.

Deaf culture together (Kannapell 1989, 1993). Overarching all four factors is attitude. Culturally Deaf people are keenly aware of other deaf people's attitudes. Without the proper attitude, one that embraces and cherishes the experience, values, and language of Deaf people, a person cannot gain entry into Deaf culture.

## Patterns of Communication

The Apache jokes mentioned earlier were based on White people's speaking behaviors. The jokes reveal that Apaches have different ways of speaking. The ethnography of communication (Hymes 1964) refers to the characteristic ways in which a group organizes its communication. This is another way to examine American Deaf culture.

Stephanie Hall (1989) described the ethnography of communication in a Deaf club in Pennsylvania. She identified several unique aspects of the communicative behavior of Deaf people in their interactions with others.

1. *Saying hello.* In order to begin a conversation, one must first get the other person's attention. With Deaf people, this is often accomplished by touching the person to whom one wants to talk. There are few restrictions on who can touch whom; if there were, communication would be impaired. As a result, Hall notes that "physical contact is so commonly a part of Deaf communication that Deaf people find it amusing and sometimes puzzling when hearing people are startled or averse to being touched" (1989, 93). When touching is not possible, such as when the person is too far away, other means of obtaining the person's attention are used: waving; stomping on the floor (not appropriate in every occasion because it distracts others); shouting the person's name[2]; or flashing the lights (again, used in restricted situations, such as a classroom, because it distracts others).

2. *Ensuring communication.* Making information available to all is an important value in Deaf culture. Sharing of personal information is more open. Deaf people make every effort to ensure that everyone is fully able to engage in conversations and

follow what is happening. Periodic checks on comprehension are common, such as "UNDERSTAND?" Deaf people are quite aware of impediments to communication in a visual language, such as poor lighting or momentary visual distractions, and will take the initiative to change the environment or pause in their conversation to ensure communication.

3. *Sharing information.* Information is a highly valued commodity in Deaf culture, perhaps because in their excursions in the hearing world—in education, employment, shopping, etc. — information is so hard to come by. Hall notes that sharing information is an affirmation of the unity of the Deaf community. Deaf people in turn often find a hearing person's attitude toward privacy to be infuriating and perplexing.

4. *Turning one's back.* Because of the value placed on sharing information, and because ASL is a visual language, there is a high value placed on maintaining eye contact in Deaf interactions. Frequently, in Deaf-hearing interactions, hearing people will fail to maintain proper eye contact (because of some visual or auditory distraction, or perhaps merely because maintaining eye contact for long periods of time seems to be uncomfortable for many hearing people); unless acquainted with the odd ways of hearing people, the Deaf person may feel slighted, or think that the hearing person is uninterested in maintaining the conversation. Naturally, in a culture that values openness of communication in a visual language, turning one's back is an insult. When circumstances make it necessary to turn one's back, rules of conversational etiquette dictate that you inform your addressee that this will happen and why.

5. *Saying good-bye.* Leave-taking in Deaf culture is always a fairly formal and lengthy affair. When Deaf people end a conversation, they explain where they are going and what they will do. They often arrange for when they will meet each other again and repeat the date and time several times. Leaving a large gathering such as the Deaf club is always a sad affair. Leaving too quickly may be misinterpreted. This, too, is a source of cross-cultural miscommunication between Deaf and hearing people. Often, a

hearing person will leave a gathering of Deaf people by quietly slipping out the door; Deaf people will wonder about this and feel that the person deliberately snuck out, perhaps because he was bored with their company.

## Deaf Literature

Literature is an important topic of study in any second language classroom, and the ASL classroom is no exception. ASL students should be exposed to the various types of literature in the Deaf community. They should learn an appreciation for the varieties of Deaf literature. ASL instructors are cautioned not to be overly restrictive in their conception of Deaf literature. To repeat what was explained in chapter 2, there is currently no commonly accepted written form for ASL. The Deaf community is a bilingual, trimodal community. Both of these facts must be taken into account when incorporating Deaf literature into the ASL instruction.

First, ASL instructors need to remember that literary works need not be recorded in writing to constitute literature. Frishberg (1988) builds a strong case for the literary status of unwritten languages, and this certainly includes ASL. As was discussed in chapter 2, most of the world's languages are unwritten. This certainly does not mean that no literary works exist in these languages. Many of the "classics" of literature—the Bible, the Greek dramas—were originally unwritten. Although ASL is still an unwritten language, there exists a long and rich history of folk literature in the language. Much of this literature has been recorded on film or videotape and can serve as an excellent source of study in the ASL classroom.

Second, the point must be made that although there are many literary works in ASL, which second language students can and should learn about, ASL is not the only language in which Deaf literature appears. Deaf writers, dramatists, and poets often use English as their medium (see, for example, the Deaf authors in Wilcox 1989). These works should be recognized as Deaf literature and incorporated into the ASL classroom. Of course, they do not provide students with examples of the literary use of ASL. They can, nevertheless, serve as eloquent testimony of Deaf identity, and of individual and cultural definition. Especially for students who have not acquired fluency in ASL, Deaf literary works in English can be invaluable.

## Oratory

Frishberg (1988) has identified three genres of ASL literature: oratory, folklore, and performance art. Oratory has a long history in ASL literature. Current examples of ASL oratorical style can be seen in religious ceremonies, dinner speeches, keynote addresses, and graduation ceremonies. Bringing oratorical literature into the ASL classroom may be rather difficult. One excellent example of oratory style that can be used in the classroom is a film of George W. Veditz (mentioned in chapter 2 in the discussion of the history of ASL). This film has been transferred to videotape and is available for viewing at the Gallaudet University library. Not only does it provide students with a glimpse of ASL oratory style, but it can also be used for class discussions about ASL and Deaf history.

## Folklore

The second style that Frishberg discusses is folklore. There is a wide variety of folklore in ASL that can be used in the ASL classroom. Examples include name signs, jokes, riddles, historical anecdotes, and ABC stories (Rutherford 1988, 1989).

ABC stories are especially useful in the second language classroom. An ABC story presents a quick narrative that is highly constrained in its structure. It is composed of only 26 words, each using the handshapes of the fingerspelled alphabet. Themes are typically taboo topics such as sex, ghost stories, or tales that mock religion. Some ABC stories have become quite famous and are now frozen, literary forms; others are created on the spot by highly skilled Deaf storytellers. Sign Media, Inc., offers an excellent videotape that captures the creativity of this kind of genre, demonstrating both the use of numbers and letters to "tell a story."

*Performance Art*

The final style discussed by Filsliberg is performance art. This includes poetry in ASL and other scripted works. Videotapes of Deaf poets performing their works are still relatively rare. However, some recordings of ASL poetry are available on videotape, such as *Deaf Heritage*, produced by the San Francisco Public Library; the *Deaf Culture* series produced and available from Sign Media, Inc.; *The Treasure*, produced by InMotion Press; and *ASL Poetry* by Dawn Sign Press.

One poem, "The Door," by Ella Mae Lentz (1995; in *The Treasure*) is a particularly eloquent example of a new genre of ASL poetry that captures the spirit of Deaf culture. It portrays hearing society's oppression of ASL and Deaf people. We present it here. (The transcription is of the English translation of the poem.)

> We were simply talking in our language of signs
> When stormed by anthem driven soldiers
> Pitched a fever by the score of their regime.
> They cuffed our hands, strangled us with iron reins.
> "Follow me! Line up! Now sit!"
> The captain, whip in hand,
> Inflicts his sentence with this command:
> Speak!
>                     "Sh-?"
> Speak!
>                     "-i-?"
> Speak!
>                     "-t?"
> Damn your chains!
> We'll pronounce our own deliverance
> And articulate our message loud and clear.
>
> And for the width of a breath
> We grant each other asylum
> Talking in our language of signs.

When they pound, pound, pound.
"Don't answer. Don't open. It's bad, don't."
The thunder rolls again.
"But I want to. I want to see.
Well maybe. I just want to see."
So step by step we succumb

Our silent agreement undone.

Come out of your dark and silent world
And join us in our bright and lovely world.

Look! Those whose ears work are signing!
Yes, but such queer speech they shape.
What waits out there?
To be fair we should see more.
Could it be they've rearranged the score?

And one by one
We go down the corridor of their sterile syntax,
Not knowing . . .

The National ASL Literature Conferences sponsored by the National Technical Institute for the Deaf (NTID) have delighted and thrilled thousands of Deaf people who flocked to the NTID campus to see performances by Deaf artists. The conferences have highlighted some of the best Deaf talent in America, ranging from plays to scholarly analysis of ASL poetry. Local communities are also hosting performances in ASL.

## Deaf Literature in English

The Deaf community is bilingual. There are many works in English by Deaf poets, playwrights, novelists, and essayists that second language students can read to become more familiar with Deaf culture and the Deaf experience.

In addition to being a wonderful source of information about Deaf culture and history in general, and a thoroughly enjoyable book, Jack Gannon's (1981) *Deaf Heritage: A Narrative History of Deaf America* is an excellent source of Deaf poetry for second language students. Of course, deaf poets have existed for centuries, and not only in the United States. One of the first deaf poets was the Frenchman, Pierre de Ronsard (1524–1585). The twentieth century can claim many great American poets who were deaf: Joseph Schuyler Long, who published a book of poems in 1908 entitled *Out of the Silence*. Dorothy Miles, born in England but a graduate of Gallaudet, published a book of poems entitled *Gestures* (1976); and Robert Smithdas, who was a deaf-blind poet. One of Smithdas's most famous poems, "Shared Beauty," is also included in the *Deaf Heritage* series. Robert Panara is not only a renowned poet in his own right, but has done perhaps more than any other individual to support and encourage Deaf poets in this country. His work is also to be found in *Deaf Heritage* and in several other published works (Panara 1987, 1970; Panara and Panara 1983).

Plays by Deaf writers include *Sign Me Alice* by Gilbert Eastman; *Tales from a Clubroom* by Eugene Bergman and Bernard Bragg; *That Makes the Two of Us* by Bernard Bragg; and *The Iliad: Play by Play,* an adaptation of Homer's epic poem by playwright and author Shanny Mow. Several of these Deaf playwrights are also accomplished actors. Bragg and Mow were longtime members of the National Theatre of the Deaf.

Ben Bahan is a Deaf activist and essayist whose works are especially useful in instilling a sense of Deaf culture in hearing students. Both humorous and profound, his essays are quite accessible to second language students. One particularly excellent article is entitled "A Night of Living Terror" (Bahan 1989a). In it, he describes a series of nightmares faced by a Deaf person—all of them capturing the spirit of Deaf identity and the power struggle that Deaf people face as they attempt to take control of their cultural destiny. The nightmares culminate with the ultimate terror of Deaf culture: One day, Deaf people may wake up and find that they have become hearing people!

## Autobiographies/Interviews on Videotape

Who can better tell the story of Deaf Culture than Deaf people? Recently there have been many excellent videotapes generated that are spreading the profound experience of the Deaf heritage. Some powerful stories can be found in Sign Media's historical series, *When the Mind Hears: A History of the Deaf*, and in *ASL Across America*, videotaped conversations by diverse Deaf individuals from different regions of the country. Dawn Pictures' series, *The Man Behind the Mask*, and Sign Enhancer's autobiography series demonstrate Deaf culture from a personal point of view. Linstok Press offers *ASL Pah!: Deaf Students' Perspectives on Their Language*, moving stories from Deaf youth who feel that their lives are being drastically changed by the cultural upheaval created by the use of ASL in their educational systems. Many other commercial and locally produced videotapes render testimony to Deaf culture and its impact on Deaf individuals in the United States.

## Summary

There are many other aspects of Deaf culture not covered in this chapter that can be used in the second language classroom. Students can learn about Deaf humor and Deaf storytelling. Perhaps during one class session, Deaf people from the community could be invited to share Deaf jokes with the students or to tell popular Deaf stories. One lesson could explore Deaf visual artists. Several lessons could be devoted to viewing and discussing works performed by the National Theatre of the Deaf, many of which are available on videotape.

Deaf cultural events afford second language students many ways to use their newly acquired language skills. Some typical events that students could attend are bowling, basketball tournaments, and holiday parties such as a Halloween dance; all of these are common events in any Deaf community.

Students studying ASL should come away with a knowledge of and respect for the values of Deaf people and their culture. They should recognize that Deaf people's lives are full and complete. Students should be willing to associate with Deaf people—why else are they learning their language?

# Notes

1.  The use of small capital letters here is meant to distinguish the ASL term from the English translation of a sign. Thus, the term HEARING, for example, is meant to represent the ASL word that differs in meaning from the English word *hearing*.

2.  Some deaf individuals have enough hearing to recognize their name when it is called. It may seem puzzling to read that Deaf people can hear. The reader is to be reminded that the term *Deaf* (with a capital D) refers to a cultural affiliation and not to a degree of hearing.

# 4

# *Teaching ASL*

## Program Design

### *Needs Assessment*

The first step in designing any type of program that will offer ASL instruction is to conduct a needs assessment. As with any second language program, an analysis of the local academic and community environment is needed to determine the following (Crandall and Bruhn 1982, 79):

- Who the learners are and why they are studying the language;
- What resources are available, including teaching materials and personnel;
- Who the teachers are and what special needs they may have;
- Where the language is to be taught; and
- How much time is available for instruction.

The administrators and faculty involved in designing an ASL program must be aware of the effect of the philosophy and approach that they choose. They also must be concerned with the community from which their student body comes. There are several questions to be considered. Will the majority of the students be expected to go directly into an interpreter education program following completion of their signed language studies? Does the anticipated student body come from a local community in which few plan to interpret professionally? Are there any preschools in the area that advocate the bicultural model of deaf education? Is there a large mainstreaming deaf education program in the local public schools that uses English signed systems exclusively? Are the people making decisions about the program aware of the educational and cultural ramifications involved in the instruction of this language? Are the policy makers aware of the learner variables (age, physical abilities, motivation, etc.) represented in the student population? Or, are they simply interested in setting up classes to accommodate the growing number of students who express an interest in "sign language"?

A needs assessment should attempt to involve all groups who have a vested interest in the students who will participate in the ASL program. The Deaf community, parents of deaf children, teachers and administrators in the public and state residential schools, practicing signed language interpreters, state legislators, and others may be affected by and may influence the ASL program. Educators will find greater acceptance and support for their program later by soliciting input from these individuals and groups during program developmental stages. Students who finish the program will eventually become a part of the local social, political, economic, and educational community. Ethnographers working in the area of cultural transmission in schools are finding that the "hidden curriculum" (or what is taught implicitly as opposed to the academic skills designated by curriculum content) has an impact on the presented information and even on culture in the classroom. Acquisition of particular skills depends not so much on individual characteristics as on the types of skills demanded by the environment (Wilcox 1982). In other words, the local community will have an effect on the outcome of the ASL program. Positive community support through a joint exploration of community values is worth pursuing.

The age of the students should be taken into consideration when designing or adapting a program. Generally, younger learners' rote memory skills can be used effectively when introducing ASL. Adults who have more advanced cognitive levels can reflect upon and analyze the target language and can organize materials in ways that will facilitate acquisition (Gleason and Pan

1988). An ASL linguistics theory course will be a desired addition for adult learners who may wish to analyze the syntax and semantics of this signed language through a comparison with spoken language linguistics. Age and cognitive differences become crucial when curricula are designed and developed.

Equally important are the personnel resources available. Chapter 5 offers criteria to consider when hiring the most important component of the ASL program—the faculty. Team teaching in the form of Deaf/hearing teams can also be considered. The success of a Deaf/hearing team in teaching English to deaf students (Humphries, Martin, and Coye 1989) certainly suggests that a similar combination could be successful for teaching ASL to hearing students.

In addition to regular resources that any adequate second language program provides (instructors, lab consultants, facilities, textbooks, and so on), a videotape component is essential. Even in the early 1980s, access to videotape equipment was often limited. This is changing. Almost every established ASL program now makes extensive use of television monitors and cameras. The equipment is necessary for the exploration and learning of this visual-gestural language. Instructors take pride in expanding their videotape collection along with their written library.

Media personnel knowledgeable in working with Deaf consultants and an extensive videotape language lab are essential ingredients to the success of any ASL program.

## Administration

In the past, signed language programs were often housed in special education or communicative disorders departments. These departments supported many classes throughout the late 1960s, 1970s, and early 1980s, when the demand for signed language instruction began to increase steadily. However, the signed language classes were often taught from a clinical/pathological point of view, and the cultural heritage of the Deaf community and the rich linguistic structure of ASL were often ignored. More recently, ASL programs have been welcomed into departments of linguistics and modern and classical languages. University administrators are aware of the scholarly research potential of ASL, especially in the area of linguistics. Individuals involved in program development have also become more knowledgeable about second language teaching methodology. They are recognizing the importance of hiring bilingual/bicultural faculty and administrators.

Policy makers must be aware of the time frame available for their course sequencing. To provide minimal instruction in any second language means offering several semesters of the language. At least one separate course on Deaf culture should be included. In addition, a holistic introductory course should be considered for adult student populations, with the course content including the history of ASL and signed systems in our country, myths and misconceptions of deafness and ASL, pioneering research on ASL linguistics, orientation to the Deaf community, and so forth. The academic arena is the proper place for discussion of the cultural and linguistic ramifications of language choices available to all deaf persons in America today.

A more sophisticated and in-depth structure, one that would adequately prepare students for a signed language interpreter education program and expose them to a general liberal arts education, should be housed in a four-year degree program of signed language studies. A full program in signed language studies should include, in addition to American Deaf culture and ASL second language instruction, courses on the linguistics of ASL, Deaf history, language contact theories, ASL literature, fingerspelling theory and prediction strategies, and sociolinguistic and psycholinguistic aspects of ASL and deafness.

As noted in chapter 2, ASL classes and programs are currently housed in associate, baccalaureate, and graduate degree programs, as well as in community colleges and technical schools. Programs are also rapidly becoming adopted in high schools, middle schools, and elementary schools. However, this astonishing growth of interest in ASL can be a cause of concern. As Gary Olsen warns, "A word of caution . . . a groundswell can be devastating if proper precautions are not taken. Without proper standardization of curriculum, instructor qualifications, and certification, this sudden spontaneity of acceptance of ASL can be devastating. ASL, as we know it today, could be drastically altered or lost" (Olsen 1988, 100).

The National Association of the Deaf (NAD) has recently established an ad hoc committee on ASL curriculum development under a branch of its organization, American Sign Language Teachers Association (ASLTA) [formerly the Sign Instructors Guidance Network (SIGN)]. The NAD recognizes that the development of standard curriculum models for both the high school and college levels is a concern of the highest priority. The organization is watching with alarm as an increasing number of ASL classes are being set up haphazardly across the nation; the organization recognizes that the United States needs curriculum guidelines for the elementary and middle school levels also. Today, no program or agency is actively directing and controlling program planning, curriculum development, placement guidelines, and articulation and evaluation of ASL instruction at all educational levels on a national scale. This places tremendous responsibility upon the local and state policy makers to guarantee that the ASL program design is coherent, protects the integrity of ASL, and is supported by resources that ensure that adequate instruction by appropriate personnel takes place.

## ASL Curriculum Design

After a needs assessment has generated guidelines for the design and structure of the ASL program, focus must be turned to the development of an appropriate curriculum.

As recently as 1982, the application of principles of second language acquisition and instruction to the teaching of signed language was a relatively new idea (Cogen and Philip 1982). Many current instructors of ASL can recall when a common way to teach signed language was by demonstrating simple signed equivalents for English words (Baker-Shenk and Cokely 1980b). Battison and Cogen (1978) recounted the structure of many ASL classes of that time.

> Typically, a basic sign vocabulary consisting of morphologically simple forms is provided, and the structure of sentences and conversations are [sic] left to the discretion of each individual student. Instruction in ASL grammar is sometimes confused with "nonverbal communication;" discussion of sentence patterns might only occur in advanced classes, where so-called idioms are introduced. Pronunciation and the "intonational" aspects of signs are often summed up in one instruction: Use a lot of facial expression. (p. 143)

In more recent years, numerous programs and individuals have set out to apply recognized methodological strategies from the second language learning field to the teaching of ASL. Signed language instruction has undergone tremendous progress in a relatively short period of time. Methodologies available to spoken language instructors have been adapted by many signed language teachers in their efforts to teach ASL effectively.

## Second Language Teaching Approaches

One of the earliest approaches used by instructors of spoken languages was the *grammar translation* approach known for its emphasis on the memorization of vocabulary and grammatical rules (O'Grady, Dobrovolsky, and Aronoff 1989). Traditionally, little attempt was made to communicate in the target language, and directions and explanations were always given in the first, or source, language (Richard-Amato 1988). This approach was used frequently by teachers of "sign language" in the 1950s and 1960s before pioneering research provided evidence that ASL was a language in its own right. Many teachers would speak in English while showing lists of signs to their classes. Students were expected to produce errorless imitations from the beginning. Needless to say, few students acquired fluency in ASL from this method.

The *audiolingual* method emphasizes using the target language, with little reference made to the source language. Language learning is viewed as a set of conditioned habits to be processed as mechanical mimicry (O'Grady, Dobrovolsky, and Aronoff 1989). This method encourages habit-forming, automatic responses through the use of memorized dialogues and patterned sentences. It is teacher-centered, and also insists on imitation and errorless reproductions of the target language (Cogen and Philip 1982). Students taught through this method are expected to see a signed word, then make a perfect reproduction of it without necessarily comprehending what they see.

The *cognitive* approach attempts to organize materials around a grammatical syllabus while allowing for meaningful practice and use of language (Richards and Rodgers 1986). Generally, it is felt that phonemes need to be learned before words, words before phrases and sentences, simple sentences before more complicated ones, and so forth (Richard-Amato 1988). The approach also emphasizes understanding and encourages the conscious selection of grammatical forms. The student's ability to create meaningful responses to new language situations is thought to be enhanced, and a functional knowledge of grammar is considered to be essential (Cogen and Philip 1982). Although students are generally encouraged to produce correct forms of the language from the first attempt (Richard-Amato 1988), inaccuracies are expected and are viewed as important components in the learning process (Cogen and Philip 1982). Linguists began rejecting the behaviorist view of language learning in the late 1950s (Cogen and Philip 1982), but it was not until the early 1980s that ASL teachers began using the rule-governed and creative cognitive approach in a widespread manner.

Most leading language acquisition and teaching theorists now support a holistic view of second language learning. Habit-forming and cognitive approaches have a role to play in language acquisition, along with functional/notional teaching methods. Teachers should be sensitive to the individual needs of students rather than to any dominant language methodology (Finocchiaro and Brumfit 1983).

Oller notes that "language users do not acquire language in terms of separate and unrelated phonemes, morphemes, words, skills, subcomponents, and so forth. We acquire language in whole contexts of communication where all of the various skills and components are at least potentially involved in acts of communication" (1989, 9). Newmark asserts that "complex bits of language are learned a whole chunk at a time . . . the language exponentiates as the number of chunks increases additively, since every complex chunk makes available a further analysis of old chunks into new elements, each still attached to the original context upon which its appropriateness depends" (1983, 49).

This belief that language can be learned through "chunks of context" gives weight to the *communicative* methodology. This approach does not look at any prescribed way of teaching—either grammatical or functional. Traditionally, methodologies have been expected to follow the direction implicit in the curricula content. A communicative methodology does not have a specific entry or exit point. Choosing directions for language learning becomes a part of the curriculum itself and involves interdependent negotiation between the students and the teacher throughout the learning process. Content of the course can be predicted within methodology only to the extent that it serves the communicative learning process of the students (Breen and Candlin 1979).

## Approaches to Teaching ASL

At one time, the typical ASL instructor was provided with two cognitively based textbooks that contributed to the expansion of ASL teaching across the country. The first, *A Basic Course in American Sign Language* (see appendix 2), emphasized a conscious awareness of the grammatical structure of the target language and provided substitution drills, transformation drills, and question-response drills (Ingram 1982). It quickly replaced the audiolingually (in this case, "visualingually") structured book that had preceded it, *A Basic Course in Manual Communication* (see appendix 2), a small picture book of signs with practice sentences organized at the end of the book.

The second offering, actually a series of textbooks and video-tapes entitled *American Sign Language* (see appendices 1 and 2), boasted of a spiraling concept in which a series of objectives required deeper and deeper levels of skill at advancing points in the curriculum (Baker-Shenk and Cokely 1980b). It also advocated an *interactive* approach to the learning of ASL, allowing the students to memorize dialogues and then "interact" while performing the dialogues. Although the series of textbooks and videotapes was embraced widely, Ingram noted that "the technique [a line-by-line analysis of that unit's dialogue] can be overdone to the point that one's command of the target language becomes mechanical rather than spontaneous"(1982, 220). Ingram also recognized, however, that the three student texts of this series "represent the highest achievement to date in the application of linguistic data and modern second language teaching theory to the design of sign language teaching materials"(1982, 219).

During the 1980s, ASL instructors became intrigued with the research being generated by ASL linguists. Verification that ASL exhibited many of the universal features of spoken languages —productivity, arbitrariness, displacement, and so on—was a source of pride and empowerment. There was great motivation to include these new linguistic findings into the signed language lesson plans being used. Teachers across the country set out to create their own linguistic-based lesson plans, with no one curriculum being used as a standard.

ASL instructors at Vista Community College in California began to assess their program's effectiveness and that of other programs across the country. The instructors found that students seemed to be learning how to use the ASL grammatical structures correctly, yet were not able to converse naturally in ASL. The students did not feel comfortable in cross-cultural interactions with Deaf individuals (Smith 1988). This concern eventually led the United States Department of Education's Fund for the Improvement of Postsecondary Education (FIPSE) to award the Vista Community College group a grant to develop a standardized ASL curriculum. The theoretical approach chosen for this postsecondary curriculum development project was the *functional/notional* approach.

Although the functional/notional approach had its roots in the 1960s, it did not begin to flourish in our country until the early 1980s. The approach places major emphasis on the communicative purpose of speech acts—the *functions* of a language (Finocchiaro and Brumfit 1983). Do you want to introduce people to one another? Do you want to invite someone to your home? Do you want to direct someone to do or not to do something? Do you want to talk about a picture, a book, a film, or someone in the room? Do you want to give sway to your creative impulses and recite a poem? Vista instructors found that this approach helped their students to interact comfortably with members of the Deaf community. The Vista curriculum guide contributes to the preservation of the integrity of ASL and has encouraged more Deaf individuals to become instructors. Vista's comfortable approach has made ASL more accessible to hearing students; yet, at the same time, it has demonstrated to them that ASL is the "subtle, elegant, powerful language of a rich, complex culture" (Smith, Lentz, and Mikos 1989, ix).

Vista's *Signing Naturally* curriculum stresses functional strategies in the form of requesting information, expressing needs or emotions, accepting or rejecting invitations, and other interpersonal communicative competencies. It also introduces grammatical structures as determined by the function of the unit being studied. There are many adaptations of the cognitive approach in the use of subskills such as pronunciation, visual comprehension, sign and facial grammar discrimination, presentation of simple sentences before more complicated ones, and so forth. Role play situations accustom the students to crosscultural adjustment skills and awareness. In other words, although *Signing Naturally*'s primarily stated approach is functional/notional, the authors recognize the value of other theories and principles. They encourage ASL instructors to extend the prepared text if this will lead to an enrichment of further interactive, communicative activities (Smith et al. 1989).

Another recent educational curriculum, *Bravo ASL! Curriculum*, published and produced by Sign Enhancers, Inc., offers a comprehensive curriculum for grades 6–12, and at the college level. Included are more than 900 pages of support materials for teachers, including comprehensive assessment tools, overhead masters and age-appropriate activities. The videotapes that accompany the curriculum are of high quality and have won several awards, including the Silver Telly Award (1993) and the 1996 International CINDY award. The linguistic samples expose students to multicultural and age variant talents. An eclectic teaching approach matches varying teaching styles and learning preferences with a functional application of language within the context of daily life events.

Although we are aware of no ASL program based exclusively on the communicative approach, we believe that many instructors have unwittingly made use of this dynamic approach at various times, particularly on days when Deaf consultants are invited into the classroom. The visible excitement generated when a friendly, dynamic user of ASL interacts freely with the students seems to boost the students' language production and comprehension tremendously. Krashen's concept of I + 1—that with the aid of context, the learner understands language that is a bit beyond his or her current level—is manifested in such a natural communicative situation (Krashen 1981).

## Articulation and Teacher Preparation

The near future holds one issue in the area of ASL curriculum design that needs to be resolved: articulation. For example, the Texas Education Agency has adopted the use of Vista's *Signing Naturally* curriculum in high schools throughout the state. Other states are doing the same (Selover 1988). As more high schools in the country accept ASL for second language credit, the use of Vista's successful functional, interactive approach to language learning may be adopted at that level. This will create articulation problems when graduating high school students enroll in a postsecondary institution and plan to continue their ASL studies, only to find that the same Vista curriculum is being offered. Perhaps the new *Bravo ASL!* curriculum will offer an alternative to the use of one standard curriculum in both high school and post-secondary levels. Other upcoming curricula being developed will assist to diversify the teaching of ASL in classrooms across the country.

As mentioned before, there is currently no agency or unit synchronizing the growth and development of ASL classes in our country. The only real hope on the horizon is that ASL instructors are becoming aware of the serious nature of the problem and are beginning to unify their efforts towards standardization and coordination of all ASL programs. The NAD is tentatively taking the lead in this huge organizational task.

For a short period of time, there was a small, but extremely encouraging resolution of the problem dealing with ASL curriculum design—a program at Western Maryland College. Through the support of another grant from the Fund for the Improvement of Postsecondary Education (FIPSE), Western Maryland offered a master's degree program to train *teachers* of ASL. It was an outstanding program that viewed the communities of Deaf and hearing people from a linguistic and cultural perspective. Students accepted into the graduate program had to demonstrate fluency in both English and ASL. Graduating students were equipped to teach ASL and the culture of Deaf people. They were also able to apply theoretical knowledge concerning the grammatical structure of ASL, Deaf culture, and foreign language teaching to facilitate students' successful acquisition of ASL. They graduated with the ability to write curricula and to develop materials to supplement a curriculum. Because this program was an excellent model and drew its student body from across the country, it has had a powerful impact on second language teaching methodology in ASL throughout our nation. Graduates from this program have gone on to help the ASL teaching community deal with the very serious articulation problem that has begun to appear across the country at every level of instruction. (This college also offered a master's program in teaching ASL/English interpretation. Neither program is now being offered.) There is a tremendous need for specialized training in signed language studies and the education of *teachers* at the master's and doctoral levels. Regular master's and doctoral programs need to take up this charge and expand appropriately.

Until recently, signed language instructors took their cues from the spoken language field, often trailing far behind in applying theory to practice. However, John Oller (1989), in a keynote address at the 1988 national convention of the Conference of Interpreter Trainers (CIT), remarked that some of the highest levels of language instruction take place in the realm of signed languages.

> Based on what little contact I have had with foreign language teaching, second language instruction, and the whole family of related enterprises concerned with language teaching, it seems to me that (sign language instructors and interpreter educators) rank right at the top in terms of the level of success achieved. You aim higher than almost any other segment of the broad class of educators involved in language instruction. Most foreign language teachers are happy if their students can just succeed in managing one side of a fairly simple conversation. You set a higher goal for yourselves and generally achieve a higher level of success than will be observed in most other language programs. Therefore, it seems to me that you people and your organization have much to offer to the language teaching profession at large. Hopefully, increasing interaction at various levels will take place and will be mutually beneficial. (pp. 1–2)

## Course Design

### Holistic Introductory Courses

As mentioned in chapter 1, it is usually necessary for incoming students to "unlearn" stereotyped myths and misconceptions about ASL and Deaf culture. An entry level ASL class will not provide an adequate avenue for the questions that typical hearing adults have regarding the Deaf community, Deaf and hard of hearing individuals, causes of deafness, and so forth.

These are questions that need to be asked and answered in what is probably their native language, spoken English. The ASL program can be enriched by offering a course, either prior to or simultaneously with the elementary ASL course, where the adult students are free to ask questions in spoken English.

This introductory course is different from an ASL language learning course. Students are permitted to use spoken language for inquiry purposes. They are situated on a "safe" linguistic and cultural base where they are free to satisfy their curiosity about this new and intriguing language. They can be mildly cautioned about the possible and very real culture shock experienced by participants of cross-cultural encounters and can make the choice to either submerge themselves into the new linguistic and cultural experience, or remain interested bystanders (Brislin 1981). If the latter alternative is chosen, they will, at any rate, be bystanders with greater understanding of a language that probably was not previously part of their linguistic consciousness.

Any person in the field of ASL instruction is aware of the astonishing increase of sophistication in the questions asked by hearing students since the 1988 revolution of the Deaf student body (and entire national Deaf community, actually) at Gallaudet University (Gannon 1989). At the same time, our inquiring students invariably bring up questions arising from their own personal experiences: If ASL is not English, why does Aunt Mary, who became deaf a few years ago, speak and sign at the same time? If ASL is the preferred language of the Deaf community, why are many of the local school districts using manually coded sign systems? And, of course, still probably the most common question asked at any gathering of persons uninitiated to ASL and deafness: Is sign language universal? In 1982, Ingram noted that "very early in ASL courses, students begin to ask about fingerspelling and other forms of sign language" (220). Teaching about the language and people who use ASL, and about those who choose not to use it, can lead to enlightened discussions regarding the status and value of ASL.

It is also important for ASL students to be aware of one of the major sociolinguistic issues in the Deaf community today: the variation and language outcome resulting from the contact between ASL and English. Lucas and Valli (1989, 13) identify a partial outline of possible language contact situations in the American Deaf community, according to participant characteristics:

- Deaf bilinguals with hearing bilinguals;
- Deaf bilinguals with deaf bilinguals;
- Deaf bilinguals with hearing spoken-English monolinguals;
- Hearing bilinguals with deaf English signers;
- Deaf bilinguals with deaf English signers;
- Deaf English signers with hearing spoken-English monolinguals;
- Deaf English signers with hearing bilinguals;
- Deaf English signers with deaf ASL monolinguals;
- Deaf bilinguals with deaf ASL monolinguals;
- Deaf ASL monolinguals with hearing bilinguals.

A holistic introduction to signed languages, of course, cannot begin to explain fully the issues created by the linguistic outcome of language contact. Students can, however, begin to comprehend the differences involved in the language preference of deaf persons in our country. They can become aware of the complex physical and mental constraints placed upon the body when they use manually coded English systems (Marmor and Petitto 1979; Supalla 1986). The academic arena is, in our opinion, the proper place for discussion of the cultural and linguistic ramifications of language choices available to all deaf persons in America today.

A holistic introductory course can serve as an excellent vehicle for instruction about the history of ASL (as discussed in chapter 1), as well as an introduction to many of the ASL researchers. Brief summaries of the pioneering work of William C. Stokoe (Stokoe et al. 1965); Klima and Bellugi's astonishing findings on the language acquisition of Deaf children (Klima and Bellugi 1979); Frishberg's folklore tales and theory of historical change (Frishberg 1975, 1988); Battison's fascinating study on lexical borrowing in ASL (Battison and Cogen 1978); Supalla and New-port's study of the morphological relationships between ASL noun and verb pairs (Supalla and Newport 1978); Padden and Humphries' revealing cultural insights (Padden and Humphries 1988); and the work of countless other researchers create high interest among adult students who have naive assumptions about the linguistics of ASL. Brief and simplified references to the linguistic and cultural works produced by respected researchers dispel from the beginning any previous misconceptions about the simplicity of ASL's grammatical structure and its community of language users.

Indeed, adult hearing learners are often amazed at the discussion of the basic phonological and morphological aspects of ASL. The visual/gestural modes of the language are, of course, vastly different from the aural/oral modes that hearing learners use in their native language. They enjoy learning how to pronounce (produce) isolated language segments and lexical items of ASL while satisfying their cognitive curiosity about this powerful visual/gestural mode of communication.

While natural environments enhance the acquisition of communicative skills, formal environments allow for the learning of explicit rules that the student can apply accurately in specific situations. Adults often respond favorably to strategies that correspond to specific learning styles they have developed over the years. They often express a preference for a structured language learning environment in place of a more natural environment, at least in the initial stages. Once they have established a solid base in the second language, they may choose an immersion program as the next step (O'Grady, Dobrovolsky, and Aronoff 1989).

## Teaching Strategies

The main function of the second language teacher is to help make the input of the target language understandable (Richard-Amato 1988). Linguistic aspects of simplified language input that appear to promote comprehension in second language learners include the following (Hatch 1979):

- Slower rate and clearer articulation to facilitate word identification, and to allow more processing time;
- More use of high frequency vocabulary, less slang, fewer idioms;
- Syntactic simplification, shorter sentences.

There is considerable evidence that codes, such as caretaker speech, foreigner-talk, and teacher-talk, are significantly "simpler" than native speaker language and clearly help make language input more comprehensible (Richard-Amato 1988; Scarcella and Krashen 1980). Throughout its lesson plans, the Vista *Signing Naturally* curriculum incorporates strategies to make the acquisition process easier for students. Role playing is used extensively to promote simplified interactive exchanges between the students. The speed of the signing, although fluent, is recognizably slower than in a normal conversation between ASL native signers.

The *spiraling* approach is another strategy that assists students in acquiring language concepts. With this approach, "materials or skills are taught in increasingly greater depth at each succeeding level of instruction. Thus certain information or skills may be introduced in a course or program and then dealt with again later in the course or in another course in the program" (Baker-Shenk and Cokely 1980b, 183).

The teaching of descriptive classifiers adapts well to the spiraling approach. ASL has a large, linguistically rich set of words known as classifiers (see chapter 2). An instructor can teach physical characteristics of the human body and clothing styles early in the sequencing of the ASL courses so that students will have the language to use when describing other people during conversational discourse. The ability to describe simple features (e.g., long, straight hair; a full beard) comes in handy at the beginning of the language learning process.

An overhead projector can be used to display an assortment of beards and hairstyles when first demonstrating body and clothing classifiers. Students imitate the signs as they are first presented to them by the instructor. They are then allowed to assume the instructor's role, taking turns at signing one of the physical features, and calling on different class members to run to the overhead and point out the feature that was just demonstrated. The students benefit from attempting to produce the classifiers correctly. They also become adept at recognizing errors in production made by their peers and can use this discrimination to self-monitor and produce their own signs correctly. The instructor offers assistance when an obvious error is produced.

Later, a variety of pictures of current clothes and hairstyles can be obtained by assigning each student to bring two magazine pictures to class—one depicting a faddish hair or clothing style, and the other depicting a more conservative style. Students can use the pictures to practice identifying others in a quick and skillful manner.

The spiraling approach to the instruction of classifiers integrates with many activities. One inductive technique that helps students learn how to identify others fluently is to assign an outside activity conducted in a site of bustling activity, perhaps a university coffee shop or nearby shopping mail. The students work in pairs. Each member of the pair will be allotted an amount of time in which to describe as many passersby as possible. Not only do the students begin speeding up their production of the identifying classifiers, but they begin to recognize intuitively which characteristics are essential to their fellow students' comprehension and which simply waste time as far as identifying descriptive information is concerned.

The *Signing Naturally* curriculum offers an interactive assignment that covers the identification of others through a more deductive manner (Smith, Lentz, and Mikos 1988). Certain norms for identifying and describing people are first pointed out, in the order that they are usually described by members of the Deaf community: gender first, followed by height, body type, hair color, hairstyle, distinctive facial features, and so on. Students are encouraged to seek confirmation that the viewer understands who is being talked about throughout the identification process.

After the norms become familiar, students are provided with structured dialogues in which identification, confirmation, correction, acknowledgment, and reconfirmation are specified responses in the grammar practices.

American Sign Language can be taught through the use of various methodologies and approaches. Even the Vista *Signing Naturally* program, which boasts of a strong interactive, functional/notional approach to language teaching, uses numerous substrategies within its daily lesson plans. For example, the student videotapes offer repetitions of newly presented words or sentences in order to aid in the correct pronunciation of complex structures, a feature typical of the audiolingual approach. The hand really can be "quicker than the eye," and this phenomenon is recognized and dealt with through the use of excellent replays. This repetitive method has been played down in recent years; researchers realize that language acquisition comes through experience, and "experience can make use of whatever is lying around handy, *including what has recently been memorized*" (Scarcella and Krashen 1980, 34).

In contrast to this audiolingual technique is the episodic hypothesis that suggests that any text or discourse will be easier to recall and to understand if it is episodically organized (Oller and Richard-Amato 1983). ASL instructors should be aware that a narrative that is organized temporally may not be sufficient to generate a strong language learning experience. "Episodic organization requires both motivation created by conflict and the logical sequencing that is necessary to good storytelling and consistent with experience" (Richard-Amato 1988, 47).

An ASL lesson can incorporate episodic organization at the simplest level. A single picture can be handed out to a group of three students. The picture reveals a conflict, such as an angry man standing beside his car that has just been demolished by a truck. One student is told to describe the picture, and another to tell what happened immediately before the picture took place. A third student makes up what happened immediately thereafter. The students are allowed time to generate sentences to practice before they tell their story to the class. Subsequent discussion would focus not only on the correct usage of ASL, but on the story sequencing and experience vicariously shared by the three students.

An episodic lesson plan can also be intensive, spiraling in and out of the curriculum through the use of sequenced narratives involving acting out, role play, and dramatization activities. The interactive approach integrates well with episodic organization. Oller (1989) suggests that the instructor and students work through the material together until they have connected all the pieces of the meaningful storyline. This can be done by presenting the episode, a rich dramatization or videotaped story. Yes/no questions and wh-questions about what just took place elicit extensive interaction among the students and the instructor. Subsequent viewings can focus on textual and underlying story details. Elaboration would depend upon the language competency level of the students. At this point, they are encouraged to imitate elements of the dialogue. Difficult linguistic forms must be kept within students' current level of development, even while the lesson plan spirals outward, with the instructor encouraging the students to "paraphrase, translate, interpolate, extrapolate, summarize, and review the textual basis in a great variety of ways" (Oller 1989, 12). Students interact extensively through the exploration of episodic, organized material.

These shared responses can be inserted effectively into the rule-governed cognitive approach, leading to a more communicative result. For example, an instructor may want to teach the certain repeated movements that often occur with verbs in ASL to indicate how long an action lasts or how often the action occurs (temporal aspects). The slow, elliptical movement (modulation) of LONG TIME is distinct from, say, the small, straight-line repeated movement of REGULARLY (Baker-Shenk and Cokely 1980a). An overhead with the various movements projected on a screen will help the instructor introduce temporal aspects. To encourage students to use the modulations accurately, the instructor asks the students to name their favorite local restaurants and how often they go there. Several students will invariably be able to use a few correct name signs used by the Deaf community. Others will not know any name signs, nor how to explain in ASL where their favorite restaurant is located. The instructor can demonstrate how to describe a restaurant and how to locate a certain setting by using local reference points. The instructor makes sure that vocabulary is expanded to cover not only the temporal modulations of the verbs, but a variety of signs needed to indicate ONCE IN A BLUE MOON, NEVER, and so on. If the instructor successfully employs interactive techniques, the students are soon comfortable with describing their favorite restaurants, even adding short anecdotes connected to recent visits. The instructor promotes intensive practice of specific language segments, yet the lesson plan is integrated into an interactive, even communicative, activity.

In the *Signing Naturally* videotaped segments where Deaf persons and hearing students are shown interacting in seemingly normal discourse situations, the students ask the Deaf models to repeat a phrase, or fingerspelled word, just as they would in real life situations. Students are implicitly given permission to misunderstand and to ask for repetition. This reduces the student's affective filter, or anxiety state (Ellis 1986). In a permissive atmosphere, students feel less anxious about not comprehending perfectly. They have witnessed models in the videotape ask someone to repeat information, and that gives them the confidence to follow suit when they, too, cannot understand.

Some methods of second language instruction specifically include a silent period during which the learner is not required to speak and is allowed to rehearse silently. ASL courses often offer visual preparation exercises before expecting the students to produce signs accurately. Hearing students are auditorily attuned to their environment and need a transition period before becoming visually oriented. Second language educators of both spoken and signed languages are realizing that the student's comprehension of a language assists his or her production.

If the ASL program does not have a separate course on the

linguistics of ASL, the faculty may want to provide students with articles about ASL grammar. For example, early in the language acquisition process, soon after the students are first exposed to the concepts of noun and verb pairs, would be a good time to pass out Supalla and Newport's article (1978) "How Many Seats in a Chair?" Because this article is difficult for the average student who has no linguistic background, the instructor may elect not to have a test on the material. Study guide questions can be provided and a separate study session may be set up where students can read and discuss the material. The instructor can either request that a reaction paper be turned in or have a short quiz on the article after it has been discussed, in English, outside the regular classroom.

Ideally, however, research materials such as this could be put into a course on the linguistics of ASL; this course should be offered soon after the students have begun to acquire parallel syntactic, pragmatic, and semantic concepts in the ASL class-room. There are many excellent research articles and books available that will fascinate students who enroll in an ASL course thinking they will learn simply manual gestures. Of course, a baccalaureate or master's degree program in signed language studies can consider offering an advanced linguistic theory course conducted in ASL.

## Course on Deaf Culture

A successful course in Deaf culture requires that the instructor have a deep understanding of culture in general and Deaf culture in particular. In the language classroom, cultural mores and behaviors can be taught both implicitly and explicitly through interactive methods.

For example, attracting a Deaf person's attention in an appropriate manner is an essential aspect of Deaf culture. People cannot talk if they are not facing one another and attuned to the visual message. An instructor can get the attention of an entire room of students implicitly by going to the light switch and flicking it off and on several times. (The videotape, *Rules of Social Interaction,* by Bienvenu and Colonomos cautions that Deaf people recognize an appropriate and inappropriate speed and frequency for this visual attention tactic.) The instructor need not make reference to the fact that this is an acceptable manner of gaining attention in the Deaf community. If the strategy is used naturally by the instructor, students will invariably resort to using it also.

The ASL classroom seating arrangement should be considered carefully. Visibility is essential for any classroom discussion. The straight rows of desks so familiar in typical university classrooms allow only a limited interaction (Hall 1966). The instructor of the ASL classroom can encourage a more interactive seating arrangement by having all students move their chairs into a semi- or full circle before the first activity of the lesson begins. Students will soon learn to enter the room and arrange their chairs appropriately, knowing that the lesson will not begin until visibility of the language is ensured.

One example of how social rules of the Deaf community can be taught explicitly involves only a chair and an effective bicultural, bilingual instructor. This exercise deals with how to get a Deaf person's attention in order to pass on information. To participate successfully in this activity, students should already have been exposed to ASL grammatical sentence structure, wh-questions, yes/no questions, negation, rhetorical questions, and conditional questions, and should have a basic command of the language. This will enable them to discuss in ASL effective and sensitive means of attention-getting behaviors.

Allow one student to assume the role of a Deaf person. This student sits in a chair centered in the front of the room, facing away from the rest of the students. The instructor will draw a line across the entire length of the blackboard. On one end of the line is a picture of a smiling face, representing the concept "acceptable." On the other end is a frowning face, representing the idea of "objectionable." One student at a time will draw a slip of paper from a pile of attention-getting strategies. On the slips of paper will be typed action commands corresponding to strategies that have been used at one time or another by hearing people to get the attention of a Deaf person:

Tap gently twice on right shoulder;
Hit left knee once, hard;
Throw keys slightly to the left of Deaf person's shoulder;
Flick light switch off and on fast six times;
Throw your shoe at Deaf person's foot;
Grab jaw of Deaf person and turn it to face yours;
Rap hard four times on back of Deaf person's chair;
Throw wadded up piece of paper at Deaf person's back;
Wave hand in Deaf person's line of vision;
Hit top of Deaf person's head with a book;
Clap loudly behind the Deaf person's back;
Stomp on the floor hard three times.

Each student will follow the printed command on the slip of paper he or she has drawn. The role of the Deaf person is played by a different classmate each time. After each command has been executed, the instructor will ask the class to agree on the placement of a mark somewhere on the continuum. For example, when discussing the tactic of stomping feet hard on the floor, some students may offer that they have seen Deaf people do this. Someone else may suggest that if there is a fire, this kind of behavior might be appropriate. The pros and cons of acceptability and inappropriateness are raised through classroom discussion. Politeness is weighed against expediency, urgency, and danger.

After the class has discussed where the chalk mark should be placed and why, the student who played the role of the Deaf person should be asked if he or she agrees with the placement before determining the final marking on the board. Oller (1979, 20) states, "No matter how much you are told or are able to infer it will undoubtedly fall short of the information that is available to the person who experienced the events in his own flesh." Sometimes a person who experiences a certain tactic will react or feel differently than the students who base their opinions on observation alone. The instructor should offer input about where the mark should be struck on the continuum only if the students fall short of grasping the cultural norm of these behaviors. Although this exercise is planned in advance by the instructor, good discussion among the students can be generated, and a communicative, interactive experience often occurs.

A follow-up to this activity could be to show the videotape, *Rules of Social Interaction,* by Bienvenu and Colonomos (see appendix 1). This tape provides an excellent overview of social interaction among Deaf people. It can be used explicitly to generate discussion that will reinforce and refine students' perceptions gained from the class activity on attention-getting strategies. It should be noted that if the Deaf culture course is taught by a native signer, culturally appropriate behaviors will also be implicitly assimilated, naturally and comfortably, through normal classroom interaction.

Another explicit activity that can be adapted for an introductory Deaf culture class is called "Stand Up and Be Counted" (Simon, Howe, and Kirschenbaum 1972). Five signs are placed around the room far enough apart for groups to form by them without crowding. The signs are labeled, "Strongly Agree," "Agree Somewhat," "Neutral," "Disagree Somewhat," and "Strongly Disagree." The instructor signs a statement dealing with Deaf cultural issues that have been discussed only superficially in class. The students move to and station themselves in front of the sign that best describes their reaction. After brief discussions among the members of each group, volunteer spokespersons from each group explain to the whole class why they have chosen that particular position. Each group expresses itself before an interactive exchange among groups is allowed. Only one person should converse at a time. Below are sample statements to which students can react:

"If there were a way, all Deaf people would choose to become hearing."

"Dancing to music is a favorite activity in the Deaf community."
"It is acceptable to grab deaf peoples' hands in order to get
their attention."

Use of this affective activity encourages students to explore cultural beliefs and behaviors instead of memorizing cultural "rules"
cited by the instructor. Students are provided the opportunity to
discuss personal experiences with their peers ("I saw a native ASL
user at the bar last weekend, dancing up a storm, so Deaf people
must like music after all," "My Deaf cousin told me that when he
was a boy, he really liked to put his hands on the piano at the state
school for the deaf and feel the vibrations during music time"),
and weigh them through critical thinking as opposed to blind acceptance.

Richard-Amato (1988) believes that during this activity the instructor should function as a facilitator, not a participant, in order
to allow the students to express their viewpoints. Students are
asked to listen thoughtfully and nonjudgmentally, clarifying others' ideas, and accepting them on their own ground, but also re-
serving the right to state their own opinions and feelings as long
as others' rights to opinions are respected. Students should ask
the instructor's opinion on a certain issue only after all students
have had a chance to express themselves fully.

Exploring the cultural values of any group can be fascinating
and confusing. Culture is not a written set of rules. It is comprised
of interpretations that one acquires, often subconsciously, to
make sense of what is going on in the world (Geertz 1973). The
classroom activity described above, conducted in ASL, opens discussion to the variations and different responses that have been
noted by students who have had at least some limited contact
with ASL users.

A follow-up to this activity can take place by inviting several
members of the Deaf community to come and serve on a classroom panel, responding to the same questions previously raised
and discussed by the students. A deeper understanding of Deaf

culture can be gained by learning directly from people who value and respond positively to their own cultural mores. The "Stand Up and Be Counted" exercise allows students to explore for themselves culturally appropriate behaviors, and consequently it can ease students into a dialogue with Deaf visitors.

A panel of Deaf discussants can also provide an opportunity for the students to note the implicit strategies used among the Deaf visitors to gain one another's attention throughout the panel discussion. A final follow-up can take place during a subsequent class period when the students discuss the attention-getting strategies favored by the Deaf visitors. Opinions about which strategies were most successful can be shared. The teacher can encourage students to remember to use those behaviors in their future interactions with deaf people. Students can also be commended on the strategies they used during the panel discussion when they successfully gained the attention of the Deaf panelists.

Numerous other cultural mores, values, and behaviors can be explored in a good Deaf culture course: introductions, leave-taking, conversational turn-taking, language code-switching, criteria for acceptance or nonacceptance in the culture, folklore and artistic sign-play, group norms, identity, and so forth. Respect and understanding for the beliefs and culture of the Deaf community can begin in the classroom through insightful instruction by a bicultural, bilingual teacher.

## Evaluation and Measurement

There are a variety of testing measurements appropriate for use in the ASL classroom. Instructors may choose to use a discrete point test that is designed to measure only one component or one skill. The students' ability to inflect a verb accurately or to produce a certain lexical item can be tested in this manner. These tests are relatively easy to design. Oller and Perkins (1978, 39) caution, however, that "because discrete point tests do not require a person to deal with language in the way he normally does while watching television, conversing with friends, or reading or writing letters, and so on, they have the potential of distorting estimates of proficiency."

Integrative tests reflect a more natural use of language than the discrete point test because the test items do not deal with language in isolation. These tests may be more difficult to design; videotaping is required to capture a permanent record of an individual's signing ability. Regardless of which type of test is chosen, however, it is often difficult to know exactly what is being tested.

Let us consider an example of a seemingly simple testing instrument. Suppose an instructor decides to test the ability of a student to imitate a native signer from a videotape. The model on the monitor would sign a simple ASL sentence, glossed here as YES-TERDAY, CARD SEND ME ("I sent a card yesterday"). The sentence would be signed once, and sufficient pause would be allowed for the student to imitate what was seen on the monitor. A camera would record the student's responses. The model would then sign exactly the same sentence as in the first instance, but execute SEND in a different direction. Following another pause of the same length, the student would copy the model again. Each time, for at least a dozen instances, the videotaped model would sign the identical sentence—except for a difference in directionality of the verb—and the student would imitate what was signed.

When grading the videotape of the students, the instructor should be aware that the test is evaluating more than the students' ability to imitate another person's signs. It is testing their short-term memory retention and their ability to determine whether to copy by using an identical or a mirrored response. In addition, the testing instrument can measure subject/object incorporation. Pronunciation of the signs in the sentence could also be scored objectively on this test.

Instructors must be aware of which elements are tested. If a task is going to be called a language test, it should "require processing that involves relating discourse to contexts of experience outside the linguistic forms per se" (Oller 1979, 407). If points are taken off for pronouncing SEND with an A-handshape instead of flat O-handshape, the instructor should clearly explain how this distinction makes a critical difference. Also, if a discrete point test is being used for convenience and ease of scoring, the students should be aware of the reason behind this choice of testing.

On the other hand, an instructor can consider Swain's (1985) argument for the importance of the role of output (in the case above, imitating what is seen on the monitor) in learning a language. Swain argues that after the meaning of the message has been comprehended, the student is able to focus on form. Therefore, it is possible that good production is a sign of good comprehension and vice versa. The above test, therefore, might be useful for measuring both comprehension and production.

Teachers can also administer tests that will not be graded. The test may be provided solely or partially for the educational value of the heightened motivation that accompanies a testing situation. If the instructor is aware of the rationale behind this testing, and the students understand the testing intent, a pseudo test can serve as an admirable educational tool.

Newell (1995) reports that there is a strong consensus among teachers of ASL that it is very important that they possess the ability to demonstrate effective and sensitive methods for evaluating students. Respondents of Newell's survey ranked this criteria very high, regardless of their self-ranking of signing ability (Native/Native-Like, Near-Native, and Advanced).

## Testing Expressive and Receptive ASL Skills

Videotape equipment offers instructors a means of obtaining an accurate record of the students' signing abilities and comprehension, and eliminates the need for written ASL.

Teachers can use silent video narratives as a means of teaching ASL grammar. In one method, the teacher chooses certain grammatical constructions to be taught, and then selects a video narrative that will be used as the teaching device. (These narratives are silent scenes that have no captions.) The students are shown the video and then asked to describe the scenes in ASL by making use of the grammatical constructions that the teacher has asked for.

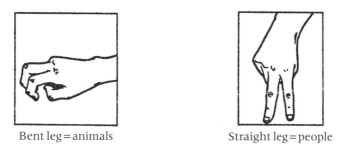

Bent leg = animals                    Straight leg = people

Figure 9:  Classifiers to distinguish animals from people

*Source:* Adapted, by permission of the publisher, from C. Baker-Shenk and D. Cokely, *American Sign Language: A Student Text, Units 1–9* (Washington, D.C.: Gallaudet University Press, 1980), 85–86.

Before the test, brief story segments are edited into a prearranged order on the master test tape. The students are placed, one at a time, in front of a videotape camera while watching the test segments on a second monitor.

Videotapes can be used, for example, to test for pronoun classifiers. One videotaped test segment shows a young boy jauntingly walking down a pathway. The students are to sign immediately what they see, remembering to make use of appropriate classifiers whenever possible. The instructor can later review the tapes of the students to grade the production, palm orientation, and path movement of the classifier selected for PERSON, taking into consideration that there are several correct ways to use this classifier to represent a person walking down a lane.

Another portion of the videotaped test could include a segment of two rabbits hopping down a lane. This segment would require that students demonstrate the proper classifiers used for animals and not those used for people (see figure 9).

The instructor can design the testing instrument so that any number of classifier referents—size, shape, pronouns, nouns, animate, inanimate, singular, plural, and so on—can be evaluated. The videotaped segments must be selected carefully so that the students will not be confused by excessive sign possibilities. Of course, the students should be told ahead of time what general grammar principles they will be expected to sign and how they will be graded (correct pronunciation, fluency, memory retention, narrative versus single sign, and so forth).

Instructors can also videotape students as they describe in ASL the details of a photograph or picture. This activity can be used as a test item for evaluating specific language points taught previously in the classroom.

A single test instrument can determine the student progress in many areas. For example, the students could be shown a picture of a double bed with brass bedposts in the middle of a vast meadow in front of a mountain range. The students will each be given a limited amount of time to describe what they see in the picture. They are videotaped while they describe the picture. The instructor may limit evaluation to simple classifier usage or award extra credit if a student makes use of other linguistic elements, such as correct locative relationships, conversational openings, or the use of rhetorical questions. For example, a student might indicate that the picture is strange and then proceed to explain why: "Wow, that sure is a strange picture. You know why? The bed's outside in the middle of a meadow!"

Cokely (1982) designed an interesting interactive arrangement that allows instructors to evaluate student progress. In this arrangement, one student interviews another. Instructors supply the necessary role-play background information to the students. During the interview, instructors can focus their evaluation on targeted vocabulary items, grammatical features, or conversational behaviors of both students. As an additional educational value, the class can use their ASL skills to discuss the interview outcome immediately afterwards.

Students should know ahead of time what they will be tested on. At the beginning level, information regarding tests (dates, times, materials, etc.) can be supplemented with written information passed out at the end of a class period. Examinations given in the advanced classes, however, should be explained in ASL only. By that time, students should know how to convey their lack of comprehension, how to ask questions, and clarify any misunderstandings, and should be aware of the cultural expectations (Hall 1989) of admitting when something has not been understood.

*Using Written Tests in the ASL Classroom*

Information dealing with articles passed out in class can be tested in a typical written-test format: essay, true/false, short answer, or multiple choice. Students receive the information in written form and answer with paper and pen. However, a dual mode approach can also be used. Test items can be signed by the instructor, and answers written by the students.

Multiple choice tests in this dual format can be used to evaluate grammatical features. An ASL instructor can design a multiple choice testing instrument by videotaping a model using correct and incorrect ASL grammatical features. Students circle a corresponding answer on the written test sheet. This type of multiple choice testing instrument can be used to test pronunciation, word choice, sentence-level grammar, discourse structure, and cultural awareness.

## Instructional Materials

ASL programs require many of the same resources as any spoken language learning center or program, except the audiolingual learning lab. In order to be effective, ASL programs must have available high quality video recording and playback facilities. In addition, the program must have a video language lab equipped with a large collection of ASL and Deaf culture videotapes and facilities for students to view tapes on an individual basis.

*Texts*

Numerous excellent textbooks are now available for use in the ASL classroom. Two have been discussed previously in this chapter and are included in the appendices; a selected listing of other ASL textbooks is also included therein.

*Videotapes*

As discussed, videotapes are a critical component of any ASL program. Several commercial videotapes about ASL and Deaf culture are now available. A partial list is included in appendix 1. Although important as educational resources, videotapes cannot substitute for face-to-face interaction with fluent language users. Few of the commercial videotapes currently available offer strategies for an interactive, communicative approach to the learning of ASL. However, an excellent functional/notional approach to teaching is provided in the Vista *Signing Naturally* tape. All the videotaped lessons are presented in ASL, without the use of voice, written English, or glosses. Many of the videotaped presentations are repeated at a normal or slower than normal rate of speed. The students purchase their own videotaped texts. Also, the *Bravo ASL!* curriculum videotapes have won many awards and provide excellent educational resources.

Other videotapes range from poorly designed vocabulary lessons to excellent ASL signing role models. Most of the commercial tapes have focused on the adult population, but many are now focusing on Deaf children. Instructors and program administrators will want to do a bit of research before purchasing commercial videotapes.

Locally produced videotapes are a good resource for language learning. The quality and format may be poor due to the lack of production-quality cameras and equipment, but these tapes can supplement an ASL curriculum with local signed dialects, diglossia, and conversational topics not provided by the commercial companies. Inviting members of the Deaf community to participate as language consultants on the video can also lead to strong ties between the students learning ASL and the people who use the language in the local Deaf community.

*Objects and Pictures*

An ASL program requires the same extensive collection of pictures and objects as any spoken second language learning program: pictures of objects and actions; sequenced story-line pictures; tinker toy construction sets (used for teaching size and shape classifiers); building blocks of various shapes and colors; doll houses and furniture; objects representing animals and people; vehicular toys; maps of countries and local geographical areas; and so on.

Objects and pictures provide nonlinguistic means of comprehension and encourage the use of "here and now" language. Pictures used regularly can be laminated for protection. Overhead transparencies can be used to present new vocabulary.

*Flashcards*

Flashcards of various designs have been marketed to spoken language learners for self-instructional purposes. Most of these cards have the target language term printed on one side with the English equivalent on the reverse side. Flashcards can be used for learning and reviewing at the most elementary levels of instruction, but they usually do not lead to interactive, communicative discourse (Gleason and Pan 1988).

The use of flashcards in teaching ASL can be as misleading as in teaching spoken languages. For example, a flashcard made for ASL instruction typically has a picture of a "frozen" sign on one side with an equivalent English gloss on the other. This leads the learner to associate the ASL word with one English word. If the word is a common object, using the flashcard may help the learner remember how to produce the sign for, say, CAT. On the other hand, if the flashcard shows a picture of a commonly used ASL verb, such as GIVE, one drawing will not be able to convey the many verbal inflections ASL contains.

The resourceful teacher can, however, make creative use of flashcards. Handshape flashcards can be used in exercises at the phonological (pronunciation) level of instruction (Bahan and Paul 1984). These can be used for "break away" exercises during a regular class or lab session. Some interactive benefits are gained from flashcard exercises because comprehension and discrimination are required when determining if the production and order of the handshape are correct or not.

The use of flashcards can go beyond the simple pronunciation

Figure 10: Example of a marked hand configuration

level. A card with a marked hand configuration (figure 10) can be shown to a pair of students. Each student is then encouraged to take turns signing words that have this particular hand configuration (e.g., HATE, MELON, MOSQUITO, TERRIBLE). McIntire (1977, 1994) has suggested that deaf children acquire unmarked handshapes more rapidly than they do marked handshapes because of the complex pronunciation of the latter. In its most general sense, markedness refers to the presence, rather than absence, of a particular linguistic feature (Crystal 1983). If McIntire's theory also applies to second language learners, then this flashcard exercise is a good one for the practice of complex handshape production and for the review of previously learned signs.

*Computers*

Most of the current, computer-designed signed and fingerspelling programs have been a disappointment. Teachers complain of the lack of resolution of the signing movements. There is an artificial quality to sign movements and transitions between signed words. Several new technologies are now available, however, that allow video to be displayed on the computer. These technologies hold great promise for ASL instruction.

One of these new technologies, videodiscs, store recorded segments much like a videotape. The difference is that information is stored sequentially on a videotape. In order to locate a specific section at the end of the tape, the user must move through the entire tape; this could take several minutes. On videodiscs, information is stored in much the same way as on a computer disk.

This enables random access of information stored anywhere on the disk. Thus, the user can locate information anywhere on the videodisc within a matter of seconds. Integrated combinations of hardware and software—jointly termed multimedia—link the images stored on the videodisc to a computer that is used to store the locations of video segments, do complex searches based on the student's input, and play the selected portion of the tape (Ambron and Hooper 1990).

CD-ROM drives are now widely available on computers. A few CD-ROM applications have appeared that present students with ASL material, including dictionaries, fingerspelling, and vocabulary. On the horizon is a new technology for delivering video and other material, called Digital Versatile Disk (DVD).

Finally, technologies for displaying video across networked computers, such as Apple QuickTime Conferencing®, will likely become the standard method of implementing video language learning labs for ASL instruction. A prototype for one such language learning lab is described in Vigil and Wilcox (1996).

Although multimedia technology has been explored in the teaching of spoken foreign languages, until recently, it has remained largely untapped for use in teaching ASL (Garrett, Noblitt, and Dominguez 1990). This is surprising because multimedia is suited for visual presentations and learning by doing. A few pioneer projects are geared toward bringing this innovative and exciting new resource to the field of ASL instruction.

# 5

## Special Considerations

In this final chapter, we will discuss several special considerations routinely reviewed by second language teachers of ASL. These will include the distinction between ASL programs and interpreting programs, teacher qualifications, and the ASL program's relationship with the Deaf community.

### ASL and Interpreter Education Programs

Much of the increase in the popularity of ASL is no doubt attributable to the increased use of signed language interpreters.

For generations, children of deaf adults (CODAs) have filled the role of interpreter for deaf family members. Although many CODAs have excellent language skills, they usually have no special training in the process or professional ethics of interpreting. Interpreting for the deaf was not considered a profession until 1964; CODAs were usually unpaid for their services. As a result, students, deaf professionals, and others had difficulty obtaining the services of a highly qualified, professional interpreter.

In 1964, a group of signed language interpreters established the national Registry of Interpreters for the Deaf (RID). Since then, the RID has worked to promote interpreting as a profession, to establish a code of ethical behavior for interpreters, to hold workshops for the training of interpreters, and to implement

112

a national evaluation system to test and certify qualified interpreters.

The profession of signed language interpreting has grown by leaps and bounds since the RID was set up. Interpreters are now recognized as professionals. Many interpreters are employed full time and work in schools, colleges, or government agencies. Others find that they can earn a living by operating on a private practice basis.

Signed language interpreter education programs are now quite common across the United States. In the early years of interpreting, there were few formal programs. Typically, people wanting to become interpreters acquired their language skills by becoming friends with a deaf person or by taking a few "sign language" courses. If they were lucky, they were also able to acquire some training in interpreting by attending workshops sponsored by RID or by a local college. In the 1970s, specialized programs were established to train people to become signed language interpreters. Most of these programs were at the associate's degree level. Soon to appear were programs that offered baccalaureate education in signed language interpreting. The current trend is for interpreter education to take place on the graduate level.

Second language students of ASL must learn the distinction between the ability to communicate in a language and the ability to interpret between two languages and two cultures. Learning ASL and studying Deaf culture enable students to communicate with Deaf people. Much more is involved in becoming an interpreter. Interpreters must, of course, be fluent in two languages. They must also be bicultural. Because interpreters will be called on to work in a wide variety of settings, they must possess a range of knowledge on several topics.

Interpreters receive training in professional ethics, including confidentiality. Specialized skills must be studied and practiced, such as consecutive interpretation (language is translated long segment by long segment); watching a deaf person sign, and voicing the message in spoken English (sign-to-voice interpreting); listening to an English spoken message and simultaneously conveying it in ASL (voice-to-sign interpreting); analyzing messages for meaning; decision-making skills; and business practices.

Often, local demand exceeds the availability of certified interpreters. In these situations, businesses, schools, agencies, and deaf people may ask ASL students to act as interpreters. Students should be made aware of this possibility. We strongly recommend that ASL students not serve as interpreters. Although it may appear to the student that someone is better than no one, this may not be true. An unqualified but well-intentioned ASL student can do more harm than good without realizing it. Often, these situations arise when the provision of a certified interpreter is not required by law (e.g., at a private physician's office, during the purchase of a car, at a bank). The complexity of the language involved in these situations is likely to lie beyond the capabilities of most students. In addition, the discourse used in these situations will typically require a level of sophistication beyond that which one learns in a language course. Certified interpreters are taught to apply techniques of text and discourse analysis to ensure that the meanings and intentions expressed in the source language are conveyed in the target language.

Of course, a background in ASL and Deaf culture is an essential prerequisite to interpreting. If they are interested in pursuing a career as interpreters, ASL students will be prime candidates for interpreter education programs.

## Teacher Qualifications

The popularity of ASL has taken everyone by surprise. As we mentioned in the introduction, ASL courses often fill as soon as they are announced. With students clamoring for more ASL classes, schools and programs often face a critical shortage of qualified ASL instructors. An unfortunate result is that ASL courses are often taught by instructors who are unqualified.

What does it take to become qualified to teach ASL as a second language? Of course, fluency in ASL is an essential prerequisite, but fluency alone is not enough. Language teachers must have

certain qualifications and skills, and teachers of ASL are no exception. As Kanda and Fleischer (1988, 192) note, "it is no longer
enough just to 'sign well' or to 'be deaf'."

Kanda and Fleischer (1988) outline six qualifications that any
ASL instructor must possess. First, ASL teachers must respect the
language and its history. They should have a sense of the role
that ASL plays in the lives of Deaf people. They should know the
details of its long history of suppression. ASL teachers must be
sensitive to the fact that they are teaching a language that, for
years, was ridiculed by hearing people and denied to Deaf people.
For the most part, Deaf people have not received formal instruction in the language they love, yet hundreds of hearing students
each semester receive college credit for studying ASL. Unless
teachers and students are aware of this inequitable situation, they
will fail to understand the essence of the language and its history.

Second, ASL teachers should feel comfortable interacting
within the Deaf community—demonstrating their fluency in
ASL, as well as their knowledge of and comfort with the culture.
Many foreign language teachers believe that it is important to
spend several years abroad, not only to perfect their language
skills, but also to get to know native users of the language. The
same is certainly true of ASL. In this respect, ASL teachers have
an advantage. They need only to travel as far as their local Deaf
club to interact with Deaf people.

As for any language, there are some ASL teachers who under-
estimate the benefits of associating with native users of the language. These teachers cut themselves off from a potential resource
for improving their language skills. If they have little contact with
the Deaf community, they will undoubtedly fail to convey to their
students a sense of respect for Deaf people. Perhaps the most important result will be that the Deaf community will have little
sense of confidence in the teacher or the program. Strong ties
between ASL programs and the Deaf community are essential.

Kanda and Fleischer's third point is that ASL teachers should
have completed formal study of the language and of educational
and pedagogical principles. At one time, it was difficult to acquire

a formal background in ASL; this is becoming less so. Today, it is possible to obtain formal training not only in ASL but also in teaching ASL. Beyond this, ASL teachers should know general principles of teaching: how to prepare lesson plans, how to make and adapt materials, how to devise and use tests, and all the other skills required of any good teacher.

Fourth, ASL teachers should be familiar with second language teaching theory and methodology. Language teaching is teaching of a very special kind. To teach a second language, it is not enough to be fluent in a language, nor even to be a good teacher; ASL teachers can learn much in this regard by studying the principles and methods used by other second language teachers. Teachers should always remain aware of students' different learning styles and personality types (Doerfert and Wilcox 1986).

Fifth, ASL teachers should be engaged in personal and professional growth and development. This is especially critical in a rapidly growing and advancing field like ASL teaching. Research brings about an ever-broadening understanding of the language; teaching materials and methods are constantly being introduced. Perhaps more than any other language teachers, ASL teachers must continue to learn.

Finally, ASL teachers are human beings first, teachers second, and teachers of ASL third. ASL teachers have a unique responsibility: They are teaching students to communicate with people who live in the same town, perhaps even the same neighborhood. They are working with students who are often attracted to the language because of a desire to "help" deaf people. Teachers must convey to students a respect for the language and the people, and they must make clear that many Deaf people neither need nor want help from hearing people. ASL instructors help bridge a language and cultural gap that has existed for hundreds of years. The qualifications described above apply to all ASL teachers. Specific qualifications can be identified for ASL teachers working in high schools, colleges and universities, or community and adult education settings. Table 3 summarizes these qualifications (Kanda and Fleischer 1988).

Table 3. Qualifications of Faculty Teaching ASL

| | High School | College/University | Community/Adult Education |
|---|---|---|---|
| Education | BA in ASL/Deaf Studies or related field | Bachelor's in ASL/Deaf Studies or related field<br><br>Master's/doctorate in ASL, Linguistics, Deaf Studies, or Education | Bilingual<br><br>Workshops/courses in adult education, curricula testing, linguistics of ASL, second language instruction<br><br>Minimum high school diploma, prefer BA |
| Certification | State teaching certificate in foreign language or social studies S.I.G.N.[1] | S.I.G.N. | State certificate in adult and/or community education |
| Fluency | Should have bilingual competency that has been tested by S.I.G.N., state credentialing examination, or other competent body of examiners. | | |
| Interaction with Deaf Community | Should be able to effectively interact with adult members of the Deaf community, displaying cultural competency; should display strong positive attitudes of respect for the language, culture, and community; "attitudinal deafness." | | |
| Other | Demonstrated competence in teaching | Minimum 5 years teaching experience<br><br>Engage in research of ASL, instructional techniques, language acquisition, etc.<br><br>Be published in the field. | Demonstrated competence in teaching |

1. Sign Instructors Guidance Network. This organization is now called the American Sign Language Teachers Association (ASLTA). See Appendix 3 for more information.

Source: Reprinted, by permission of the publisher, from J. Kanda and L. Fleischer, "Who is qualified to teach American Sign Language?" Sign Language Studies 59 (1988): 189.

# The ASL Program and the Deaf Community

ASL students do not have to travel to foreign countries to interact with ASL users. Every large town has a Deaf community that can serve as an excellent resource for ASL second language students. This section will describe ways in which students can gain access to the Deaf community.

### Bringing the Deaf Community into the Classroom

The second language teaching profession recognizes that the amount of comprehensible input necessary to achieve even moderate levels of proficiency has been seriously underestimated (Krashen 1981). In order to increase the amount of ASL used in the classroom, the ideal and obvious first choice is to hire a qualified Deaf instructor. This provides daily interaction with a member of the Deaf community and eliminates one of the most serious causes of fossilization in interlanguage development—the lack of native or native-like language models (Selinker and Lamendella 1978).

In most communities, there are Deaf people who are either already qualified or who could, with adequate supervision, learn the necessary skills to teach ASL courses. This is especially true if the Vista *Signing Naturally* or *Bravo! ASL* curricula are used in the programs.

Another way that Deaf people can be brought into the classroom is by offering lab sections as a supplement to the ASL classes. This seems to be a popular method in many ASL programs and, handled correctly, can certainly provide students with a valuable experience. The lab should complement the ASL course. The lab instructor and the course instructor should jointly plan activities that will reinforce lessons or concepts learned in the classroom. A lab section should not be considered simply a time for students to get together and converse with a Deaf person. If students want to have time to converse freely in ASL, they should be encouraged to do this by entering the Deaf community.

The lab should be an integral part of the ASL program and the lab instructor an important member of the ASL faculty. If the ASL program is large enough to have several faculty members, each should be involved in planning lab activities. Conversely, the lab instructor should be included in meetings at which curricular issues will be discussed.

Purposeful, interactive language can be fostered through the use of videotaped dialogue journals exchanged between students and members of the Deaf community, between students in separate classes, and between students and teachers. Topics can be selected by the students or by the Deaf partner. Accuracy is not considered important unless errors interfere with communication (Staton 1983). The videotaped journal is modeled after face-to-face communication; the key components in the taped journals are those commonly found in everyday conversations. Crucial for language learning is that there be a purpose to the communicative event.

The most exciting moments in the classroom often occur when members of the Deaf community visit and interact with the students. How well this interaction succeeds depends on several factors. Students who are rarely exposed to Deaf native signers may feel intimidated and nervous about the visits. This is another reason for hiring a qualified Deaf instructor. When interaction with Deaf signers is a regular part of the curriculum, students look forward to the opportunities to practice, in a natural manner, the cultural mores and grammatical structures that have been taught in formal class lessons.

Prior planning can help to make visits by Deaf people an effective learning experience, comfortable for students and visitors alike. Students should be told in advance that Deaf visitors will be coming. They should know what the session for the day will involve. This will allow them to prepare by practicing the lesson and by reviewing any specific vocabulary needed for the class. The students should be reminded to greet Deaf visitors when they arrive, using appropriate cultural behaviors to help the visitors feel comfortable in the classroom.

This cultural greeting can include remaining standing, and

conversing in ASL until most people have arrived. Each student should try to extend a personal greeting to visitors by facing them, looking directly into their eyes, and welcoming them in ASL. The greeting can include an affectionate, friendly hug if the Deaf person is a familiar face in the classroom.

The Deaf visitors should also be told in advance what will be expected of them. If asked to demonstrate something, such as an ABC story or an individual narrative, the visitor should understand the format of the lesson plan and the reason for studying this particular aspect of ASL. Visitors should also know the proficiency level of the students. Another important note is that teachers and program administrators must remember that Deaf visitors should always be reimbursed for their time and expertise.

## The ASL Learner Outside of the Classroom

Another way that ASL students can meet and interact with Deaf people is for them to enter the Deaf community. We do not mean that ASL students can or should attempt to be accepted into the Deaf culture. Rather, we mean that ASL students can make Deaf friends and attend Deaf cultural events.

Teachers of ASL should avoid sending their whole class to a Deaf club meeting. This would probably be uncomfortable for the students and might cause the club members to resent the intrusion. There are other appropriate events where groups of students will be welcomed. Traveling theaters of the Deaf frequently make appearances in large American cities. After a performance, cast members often join local Deaf people and their hearing friends for refreshments and conversation. Local Deaf athletic groups sponsor basketball and volleyball tournaments and usually welcome hearing students to these public events. Silent potluck dinners— "signing suppers"—are a favorite way to get together in many Deaf communities. Students are often welcomed at these casual social gatherings. If ASL students genuinely hope to get to know Deaf people better, and not just use them as language models, it is almost inevitable that two people with common interests will become friends, regardless of the student's own non-Deaf status.

Students who are asked to interpret ASL before they achieve interpreting fluency and knowledge can inquire about possible interpreting resources, such as local interpreting referral centers and interpreting chapters. The Registry of Interpreters for the Deaf annually publishes a national registry of certified interpreters. It also provides a list of interpreting referral centers. These are excellent resources for Deaf and hearing people who need to locate a certified interpreter.

The most important task of the ASL learner outside the classroom, though, is to display respect for ASL and its users. By nurturing the relationship between the Deaf community and the ASL classroom, hearing people will be allowed to enter, and perhaps share, the language and way of life of Deaf people.

# Appendix 1

## Selected Videotapes on American Sign Language and Deaf Culture

**Dawn Sign Press**
*ASL Poetry: Selected Works of Clayton Valli*
*Signing Naturally* (a five-volume videotape series)

**Gallaudet University Press**
*Deaf Mosaic's Deaf President Now! Revolution*
*Deaf Mosaic's Deaf Way, Part One*
*Deaf Mosaic's Deaf Way, Part Two*
*Deaf Mosaic's DPN: The Power and the Promise*

**InMotion Press**
*The Treasure* (Poems by Ella Mae Lentz)

**Multi-Media Evangelism, Inc.**
*The Video Dictionary of ASL Signs*

**Sign-A-Vision, Inc.**
*Visual Tales* (a five-volume videotape set)

**Sign Enhancers, Inc.**
*ASL Interpreting/Transliterating*

## Sign Media, Inc.

*American Sign Language—"The Green Books"* (a six-volume videotape set)

*American Sign Language Phrase Book* (a three-volume videotape series)

*ASL Across America* (Albuquerque, Detroit, Philadelphia, San Francisco, Seattle, St. Paul)

*ASL Numbers: Developing Your Skills* (a three-volume videotape series)

*High Five: Fables and Fairy Tales* (a five-volume videotape set)

*An Introduction to American Deaf Culture* (a five-volume videotape series)

*An Introduction to the Deaf Community*

*Poetry in Motion* (a videotape series)

*Selected Signs Around the World* (nine 30-minute videotapes, each featuring a different country) featuring Patrick Graybill, Clayton Valli, and Debbie Rennie.

## T. J. Publishers

*A Basic Course in American Sign Language Videotapes* (a four-volume videotape series)

*From Mime to Sign* (a three-volume videotape series)

Author's Note: See Appendix 3 for the full address of each publisher.

# Appendix 2

## Selected Books on American Sign Language and Deaf Culture

**Gallaudet University Press**

*American Sign Language—"The Green Books"*
   by Charlotte Baker-Shenk and Dennis Cokely (a series of textbooks and guides for teachers and students)
*Angels and Outcasts: An Anthology of Deaf Characters in Literature*
   by Trent Batson and Eugene Bergman, eds.
*At Home Among Strangers*
   by Jerome D. Schein
*Conversational Sign Language II*
   by Willard Madsen
*Dancing Without Music: Deafness in America*
   by Beryl Lieff Benderly
*A Deaf Adult Speaks Out*
   by Leo M. Jacobs
*Deaf History Unveiled: Interpretations from the New Scholarship*
   by John V. Van Cleve, ed.
*Deaf President Now!: The 1988 Revolution at Gallaudet University*
   by John B. Christiansen and Sharon N. Barnartt
*Gallaudet Survival Guide to Signing*
   by Leonard G. Lane
*Intermediate Conversational Sign Language*
   by Willard Madsen

*Language in Motion: Exploring the Nature of Sign*
by Jerome D. Schein and David A. Stewart
*Multicultural Aspects of Sociolinguistics in Deaf Communities*
by Ceil Lucas, ed.
*Never the Twain Shall Meet: Bell, Gallaudet, and the Communications Debate*
by Richard Winefield
*No Walls of Stone: An Anthology of Literature by Deaf and Hard of Hearing Writers*
by Jill Jepson, ed.
*The Other Side of Silence: Sign Language and the Deaf Community in America*
by Arden Neisser
*A Place of Their Own: Creating the Deaf Community in America*
by John V. Van Cleve and Barry A. Crouch
*The Politics of Deafness*
by Owen Wrigley
*Seeing Language in Sign: The Work of William C. Stokoe*
by Jane Maher
*Signs of the Times*
by Edgar H. Shroyer
*Sociolinguistics in Deaf Communities*
by Ceil Lucas, ed.
*The Week the World Heard Gallaudet*
by Jack R. Gannon

## HarperPerennial, HarperCollins Publishers

*Seeing Voices: A Journey into the World of the Deaf*
by Oliver Sacks

## Harvard University Press

*Deaf in America: Voices from a Culture*
by Carol Padden and Tom Humphries
*Mother Father Deaf*
by Paul Preston

*The Signs of Language*
  by Edward S. Klima and Ursula Bellugi

## Linstok Press

*American Deaf Culture: An Anthology*
  by Sherman Wilcox, ed.
*Language Choice—Identity Choice*
  by Barbara Kannapell
*Sign Language Studies Special Issue (#59): Academic Acceptance
  of American Sign Language*
  by Sherman Wilcox, ed.

## McGraw-Hill

*Gallaudet Encyclopedia of Deaf People and Deafness*
  by John V. Van Cleve, ed.

## National Association of the Deaf

*A Basic Course in Manual Communication*
  by Communicative Skills Program
*Deaf Heritage: A History of Deaf America*
  by Jack R. Gannon
*Deafness: 1993–2013*
  by Mervin Garretson, ed.
*Eyes, Hands, Voices: Communication Issues Among Deaf People*
  by Mervin Garretson, ed.
*Perspectives on Deafness: a Deaf American Monograph*
  by Mervin Garretson, ed.
*Teaching ASL as a Second/Foreign Language: Proceedings of the Third
  National Symposium on Sign Language Research and Teaching*
  (two-volume set)
  by Frank Caccamise, Mervin Garretson, and Ursula
  Bellugi, eds.
*Viewpoints on Deafness: A Deaf American Monograph*
  by Mervin Garretson, ed.

## Prentice Hall

*Learning American Sign Language*
   by Tom Humphries and Carol Padden

## Sign Media, Inc.

*American Sign Language Phrase Book*
   by Lou Fant

## T. J. Publishers

*A Basic Course in American Sign Language*
   by Carol Padden, Tom Humphries, and Terrence O'Rourke
*From Mime to Sign*
   by Gilbert C. Eastman, with Martin Noretsky and Sharon
   Censoplano

## Vintage Books, Random House, Inc.

*The Mask of Benevolence: Disabling the Deaf Community*
   by Harlan Lane

Author's Note: See Appendix 3 for the full address of each publisher.

# Appendix 3

## *Deafness-Related Organizations and Publishers*

American Sign Language
  Teachers Association—ASLTA
  (formerly the Sign Instructors
  Guidance Network—S.I.G.N.)
% National Association of the
  Deaf
814 Thayer Avenue
Silver Spring, MD 20910-4500


Dawn Sign Press
6130 Nancy Ridge Drive
San Diego, CA 92121-3223


Gallaudet University Press
800 Florida Avenue N.E.
Washington, DC 20002-3695


HarperPerennial
HarperCollins Publishers
10 East 53rd. Street
New York, NY 10022-5299

Harvard University Press
79 Garden Street
Cambridge, MA 02138-1499


InMotion Press
2625 Alcatraz Avenue #324
Berkeley, CA 94705


Linstok Press, Inc.
4020 Blackburn Lane
Burtonsville, MD 20866


Multi-Media Evangelism, Inc.
1335 S. Providence Road
Richmond, VA 23236


National Association of the Deaf
814 Thayer Avenue
Silver Spring, MD 20910-4500


National Technical Institute for
  the Deaf
One Lomb Memorial Drive
Rochester, NY 14623-0887

Prentice Hall, Simon and Schuster
  Secondary Division
113 Sylvan Avenue
Englewood Cliffs, NJ 07632

Registry of Interpreters for the
  Deaf
8630 Fenton Street
Suite 324
Silver Spring, MD 20910

Self Help for Hard of Hearing
  People
7910 Woodmont Avenue
Suite 1200
Bethesda, MD 20814

Sign-A-Vision
P.O. Box 30580
Seattle, WA 98103

Sign Enhancers, Inc.
1535 State Street
Salem, OR 97301-4255

Sign Media, Inc.
4020 Blackburn Lane
Burtonsville, MD 20866

Silent Network
6363 Sunset Boulevard
Suite 930-B
Hollywood, CA 90028

T. J. Publishers
817 Silver Spring Avenue
Suite 206
Silver Spring, MD 20910

Vintage Books, Random
  House, Inc.
201 East 50th Street
Suite 22
New York, NY 10022

Vista Community College
2020 Milvia Street
Berkeley, CA 94704

Western Maryland College
400 Hahn Street
Westminster, MD 21157

# Appendix 4

## Colleges and Universities That Accept ASL as Partial or Complete Fulfillment of Foreign Language Credits

Abilene Christian University
American University
Arizona State University
Baylor University
Brigham Young University
Brown University
California State University (Fresno)
California State University (Hayward)
California State University (Northridge)
California State University (San Marcos)
Catholic University
Centralia College
College of Staten Island
Dallas Baptist University
East Central Oklahoma State University
East Texas State University
Garner Webb University
Georgetown University
George Washington University
Hardin-Simmons University
Harvard University

Houston Baptist University
Howard Payne University
Indiana University
Lamar University
Lubbock Christian University
Madonna University
Mary Hardin Baylor University
Massachusetts Institute of Technology
Michigan State University
Northeastern University
Oklahoma Baptist University
Oklahoma State University
Pacific Lutheran University
Purdue University
Southwest Texas State University
State University of New York
Stephen F. Austin University
Texas Technical University
Texas Wesleyan University
Texas Woman's University
Trinity University
University of Alaska (Fairbanks)
University of Arkansas (Little Rock)

University of California at
   Berkeley
University of California at Davis
University of California at
   San Diego
University of Central Florida
University of Chicago
University of Colorado at Boulder
University of Hawaii (Manoa)
University of Iceland
University of Massachusetts
University of Minnesota
University of Nebraska (Lincoln)
University of Nevada (Reno)

University of New Hampshire
   (Durham)
University of New Hampshire
   (Manchester)
University of New Mexico
   (Albuquerque)
University of Rochester
University of Southern California
University of South Florida
University of Texas at Austin
University of Washington
William Rainey Harper College
Yale University

# References

Akmajian, A., R. A. Demers, and R. M. Harnish. 1984. *Linguistics: An introduction to language and communication*. Cambridge: MIT Press.

Ambron, S., and K. Hooper. 1990. *Learning with interactive multimedia: Developing and using multimedia tools in education*. Redmond, Wash.: Microsoft Press.

Bahan, B. 1989a. A night of living terror. In *American Deaf culture: An anthology*, ed. S. Wilcox. Silver Spring, Md.: Linstok Press.

———. 1989b. Notes from a "seeing person." In *American Deaf culture: An anthology*, ed. S. Wilcox. Silver Spring, Md.: Linstok Press.

———. 1989c. Total communication—a total farce. In *American Deaf culture: An anthology*, ed. S. Wilcox. Silver Spring, Md.: Linstok Press.

Bahan, B., and F. Paul. 1984. *American Sign Language handshape cards*. San Diego: Dawn Sign Press.

Baker-Shenk, C., and D. Cokely. 1980a. *American Sign Language: A student text. Units 1–9*. Washington, D.C.: Gallaudet University Press.

———. 1980b. *American Sign Language: A teacher's resource text on curriculum, methods, and evaluation*. Washington, D.C.: Gallaudet University Press.

———. 1980c. *American Sign Language: A teacher's resource text on grammar and culture*. Washington, D.C.: Gallaudet University Press.

Baron, N. S. 1981. *Speech, writing, and sign*. Bloomington, Ind.: Indiana University Press.

Basso, K. 1979. *Portraits of "The Whiteman": Linguistic play and cultural symbols among the Western Apache*. Cambridge: Cambridge University Press.

133

Battison, R. 1978. *Lexical borrowing in American Sign Language.* Silver Spring, Md.: Linstok Press.

Battison, R., and M. Carter, Jr. 1982. The academic status of sign language. In *Teaching American Sign Language as a second/foreign language: Proceedings of the third national symposium on sign language research and teaching,* ed. F. Caccamise, M. Garretson, and U. Bellugi. Silver Spring, Md.: National Association of the Deaf.

Battison, R., and C. Cogen. 1978. The implications of teaching ASL as a second language. In *ASL in a bilingual/bicultural context: Proceedings from the second national symposium on sign language research and teaching,* ed. F. Caccamise and D. Hicks. Silver Spring, Md.: National Association of the Deaf.

Bellugi, U., and M. Studdert-Kennedy, eds. 1980. *Signed and spoken language: Biological constraints on linguistic form.* Weinheim, Germany: Verlag Chemie.

Breen, M., and C. Candlin. 1979. Essentials of a communicative curriculum. *Applied Linguistics* 1(2): 90–112.

Brislin, R. 1981. *Cross-cultural encounters: Face-to-face interaction.* New York: Pergamon.

Bugos, T. J. 1980. Defending the FL requirement in the liberal arts curriculum. *Foreign Language Annals* 13(4): 301–306.

Cogen, C., and M. J. Philip. 1982. On teaching ASL as a second language: The cognitive method. In *Teaching American Sign Language as a second/foreign language: Proceedings of the third national symposium on sign language research and teaching,* ed. F. Caccamise, M. Garretson, and U. Bellugi. Silver Spring, Md.: National Association of the Deaf.

Cokely, D. 1982. A diagnostic approach to assessing American Sign Language (ASL) in the classroom. In *Teaching American Sign Language as a second/foreign language: Proceedings of the third national symposium on sign language research and teaching,* ed. F. Caccamise, M. Garretson, and U. Bellugi. Silver Spring, Md.: National Association of the Deaf.

––––––. 1983. When is a pidgin not a pidgin? An alternative analysis of the ASL-English contact situation. *Sign Language Studies* 38: 1–24.

Crandall, J., and T. Bruhn. 1982. Developing an effective language teaching curriculum. In *Teaching American Sign Language as a second/foreign language: Proceedings of the third national symposium on sign language research and teaching,* ed. F. Caccamise, M. Garretson, and U. Bellugi. Silver Spring, Md.: National Association of the Deaf.

Crystal, D. 1983. *A first dictionary of linguistics and phonetics.* 2d ed. London: Ebenezer Baylis and Son Limited.

Desloges, P. 1779. *Observations d'un sourd et muet sur "un cours elementaire d'education des sourds et muets."* Paris: Morin.

Doerfert, K., and S. Wilcox. 1986. Meeting students' affective needs: Personality types and learning preferences. *Journal of Interpretation* 3: 35–45.

Ellis, R. 1986. *Understanding second language acquisition.* Oxford: Oxford University Press.

Finocchiaro, M., and C. Brumfit. 1983. *The functional-notional approach: From theory to practice.* New York: Oxford University Press.

Forestal, L. Forthcoming. Contemporary trends in American Sign Language. In *Deafness: A Deaf American monograph,* ed. M. D. Garretson. Silver Spring, Md.: National Association of the Deaf.

Frishberg, N. 1975. Arbitrariness and iconicity: Historical change in American Sign Language. *Language* 51: 676–710.

———. 1988. Signers of tales: The case for literary status of an unwritten language. *Sign Language Studies* 59: 149–169.

Fromkin, V. A. 1988. Sign languages: Evidence for language universals and the linguistic capacity of the human brain. *Sign Language Studies* 59: 115–127.

Gannon, J. 1981. *Deaf heritage: A narrative history of Deaf America.* Silver Spring, Md.: National Association of the Deaf.

———. 1989. *The week the world heard Gallaudet.* Washington, D.C.: Gallaudet University Press.

Garrett, N., J. Noblitt, and F. Dominguez. 1990. Computers in foreign language teaching and research: A "new humanism": Part 1. *EDUCOM Review* (spring): 36–49.

Geertz, C. 1973. Person, time, and conduct in Bali. In *The interpretation of cultures: selected essays.* New York: Basic Books.

———. 1983. From the native's point of view: On the nature of anthropological understanding. In *Local knowledge: Further essays in interpretive anthropology.* New York: Basic Books.

Gleason, J., and B. Pan. 1988. Maintaining foreign language skills. In *You can take it with you: Helping students maintain foreign language skills beyond the classroom,* ed. J. Gleason. ERIC/CAL Language in Education Series. Englewood Cliffs, N.J.: Prentice-Hall Regents and the Center for Applied Linguistics.

Goodenough, W. 1957. Cultural anthropology and linguistics. In *Report of the seventh annual round table on linguistics and language study,* ed. P. Garvin. Georgetown University Monograph Series on Language and Linguistics, no. 9. Washington, D.C.: Georgetown University.

Grahn, J. 1984. *Another mother tongue: Gay words, gay worlds.* Boston: Beacon Press.

Groce, N. 1985. *Everyone here spoke sign language.* Cambridge: Harvard University Press.

Grosjean, F. 1982. *Life with two languages: An introduction to bilingualism.* Cambridge: Harvard University Press.

———. 1987. Sociolinguistics: Bilingualism. In *Gallaudet encyclopedia of deaf people and deafness,* ed J. V. Van Cleve. New York: McGraw-Hill.

Gumperz, J. J., and E. Hernandez-Chavez. 1971. Cognitive aspects of bilingualism. In *Language use and language change,* ed. W. H. Whiteley. London: Oxford University Press.

Haiman, J. 1985. *Iconicity in syntax.* Amsterdam: John Benjamins.

Hall, E. T. 1966. *The hidden dimension.* New York: Doubleday.

Hall, S. 1989. Train-Gone-Sorry: The etiquette of social conversations in American Sign Language. In *American Deaf culture: An anthology,* ed. S. Wilcox. Silver Spring, Md.: Linstok Press.

Hatch, E. 1979. Apply with caution. *Studies in Second Language Acquisition* 2: 123–143.

Holt, J., and S. Hotto. 1994. *Demographic aspects of hearing impairment: Questions and answers.* 3d ed. Washington, D.C.: Center for Assessment and Demographic Studies, Gallaudet University.

Humphries, T., B. Martin, and T. Coye. 1989. A bilingual, bicultural approach to teaching English (How two hearies and a deafie got together to teach English). In *American Deaf culture: An anthology,* ed. S. Wilcox. Silver Spring, Md.: Linstok Press.

Humphries, T., C. Padden, and T. J. O'Rourke. 1980. *A basic course in American Sign Language.* Silver Spring, Md.: T. J. Publishers.

Hymes, D. 1964. Towards ethnographies of communication. In *The ethnography of communication,* ed. J. J. Gumperz and D. Hymes. Washington, D.C.: American Anthropological Association.

Ingram, R. 1982. A review of some current sign language materials. In *Teaching American Sign Language as a second/foreign language: Proceedings of the third national symposium on sign language research and teaching,* ed. F. Caccamise, M. Garretson, and U. Bellugi. Silver Spring, Md.: National Association of the Deaf.

Johnson, R. E. 1990. Distinctive features for handshapes in American Sign Language. Paper presented at the Third International Conference on Theoretical Issues in Sign Language Research, Boston, Massachusetts.

Johnson, R. E., and S. K. Liddell. 1984. Structural diversity in the American Sign Language lexicon. In *Papers from the parasession on lexical semantics,* ed. D. Testen, V. Mishra, and J. Drogo. Chicago: Chicago Linguistics Society.

Kanda, J., and L. Fleischer. 1988. Who is qualified to teach American Sign Language? *Sign Language Studies* 59: 183–194.

Kannapell, B. 1987. Sociolinguistics: Language attitudes. In *Gallaudet encyclopedia of deaf people and deafness*, ed. J. V. Van Cleve. New York: McGraw-Hill.

———. 1989. Inside the Deaf community. In *American Deaf culture: An anthology*, ed. S. Wilcox. Silver Spring, Md.: Linstok Press.

——— 1993. *Language choice, identity choice.* Silver Spring, Md.: Linstok Press.

Klima, E., and U. Bellugi. 1979. *The signs of language.* Cambridge: Harvard University Press.

Krashen, S. 1981. *Second language acquisition and second language learning.* Oxford: Pergamon Press.

Lane, H. 1980. A chronology of the oppression of sign language in France and the United States. In *Recent perspectives on American Sign Language*, ed. H. Lane and F. Grosjean. Hillsdale, N.J.: Lawrence Erlbaum.

———. 1984. *When the mind hears: A history of the deaf.* New York: Random House.

———. 1987. Sign language, American: History. In *Gallaudet encyclopedia of deaf people and deafness*, ed. J. V. Van Cleve. New York: McGraw-Hill.

Lane, H., P. Boyes-Braem, and U. Bellugi. 1976. Preliminaries to a distinctive feature analysis of handshapes in American Sign Language. *Cognitive Psychology* 8: 263–289.

Lentz, E. 1995. The door. In *The treasure* (Poems by Ella Mae Lentz). Berkeley: InMotion Press.

Liddell, S. K. 1984. THINK and BELIEVE: Sequentiality in American Sign Language signs. *Language* 60: 372–399.

Liddell, S. K., and R. E. Johnson. 1989. American Sign Language: The phonological base. *Sign Language Studies* 64: 195–277.

Lucas, C., and C. Valli. 1989. Variation and language contact. In *The sociolinguistics of the Deaf community*, ed. C. Lucas. San Diego: Academic Press.

Marmor, G., and L. Petitto. 1979. Simultaneous communication in the classroom: How well is English grammar represented? *Sign Language Studies* 23: 99–136.

McIntire, M. 1977. The acquisition of American Sign Language hand configurations. *Sign Language Studies* 16: 247–266.

———. 1994. The acquisition of American Sign Language hand configurations. In *The acquisition of American Sign Language hand configurations*, ed. M. McIntire. Silver Spring, Md.: Linstok Press.

McIntire, M., and J. S. Reilly. 1988. Nonmanual behaviors in L1 and L2 learners of American Sign Language. *Sign Language Studies* 61: 351–375.

Moody, W. 1987. Pierre Desloges. In *Gallaudet encyclopedia of deaf people and deafness*, ed. J. V. Van Cleve. New York: McGraw-Hill.

Nash, J. E. 1987. Policy and practice in the American Sign Language community. *International Journal of the Sociology of Language* 68: 7–22.

Newell, W. J. 1995. Competencies important to teaching ASL: Perceptions between groups. *Sign Language Studies* 89: 303–330.

Newkirk, D. 1987. *Architect: Final version (SignFont handbook)*. San Diego: Emerson and Stern Associates.

Newmark, L. 1983. How not to interfere with language learning. In *Methods that work: A smorgasbord of ideas for language teachers*, ed. J. Oller and P. Richard-Amato. Rowley, Mass.: Newbury House.

O'Grady, W., M. Dobrovolsky, and M. Aronoff. 1989. *Contemporary linguistics: An introduction*. New York: St. Martin's Press.

Oller, J. 1979. *Language tests at school*. London: Longman.

————. 1989. Making sense in interpreter education programs: Evaluation. In *New dimensions in interpreter education: Evaluation and critique*, ed. S. Wilcox. Proceedings of the Sixth Annual Convention of Interpreter Trainers, July 13–17, 1988, Cedar, Michigan.

Oller, J., and K. Perkins. 1978. *Language in education: Testing the tests*. Rowley, Mass.: Newbury House.

Oller, J., and P. Richard-Amato. 1983. Some working ideas for language teaching. In *Methods that work: A smorgasbord of ideas for language teachers*, ed. J. Oller and P. Richard-Amato. Rowley, Mass.: Newbury House.

Olsen, G. 1988. Acceptance of American Sign Language: An American groundswell. *Sign Language Studies* 59: 107–108.

Padden, C. 1987. Sign languages: American. In *Gallaudet encyclopedia of deaf people and deafness*, ed. J. V. Van Cleve. New York: McGraw-Hill.

Padden, C., and T. Humphries. 1988. *Deaf in America: Voices from a culture*. Cambridge: Harvard University Press.

Panara, R. 1970. The Deaf writer in America: From colonial times to 1970. Parts 1 and 2. *American Annals of the Deaf* 115: 509–513, 673–679.

————. 1987. Literature, writers in. In *Gallaudet encyclopedia of deaf people and deafness*, ed. J. V. Van Cleve. New York: McGraw-Hill.

Panara, R., and J. Panara. 1983. *Great Deaf Americans*. Silver Spring, Md.: T. J. Publishers.

Patterson-Rudolph, C. 1993. *Petroglyphs and Pueblo myths of the Rio Grande*. Albuquerque: Avanyu Publishing.

Richard-Amato, P. 1988. *Making it happen: Interaction in the second language classroom*. White Plains, N.Y.: Longman.

Richards, J., and T. Rodgers. 1986. *Approaches and methods in language teaching: A description and analysis*. New York: Cambridge University Press.

Rutherford, S. D. 1988. The culture of American Deaf people. *Sign Language Studies* 59: 129–147.

———. 1989. Funny in deaf, not in hearing. In *American Deaf culture: An anthology*, ed. S. Wilcox. Silver Spring, Md.: Linstok Press.

Sacks, O. 1989. *Seeing voices. A journey into the world of the deaf.* New York: HarperPerennial, HarperCollins Publishers.

Sampson, G. 1985. *Writing systems: A linguistic introduction.* Stanford: Stanford University Press.

Scarcella, R., and S. Krashen. 1980. *Research in second language acquisition.* Rowley, Mass.: Newbury House.

Selinker, L., and J. Lamendella. 1978. Fossilization in interlanguage. In *On TESOL '78: EFL policies, programs, practices*, ed. C. Blatchford and J. Schachter. Washington, D.C.: Teachers of English to Speakers of Other Languages.

Selover, P. 1988. American Sign Language in the high school system. *Sign Language Studies* 59: 205–212.

Simon, S., L. Howe, and H. Kirschenbaum. 1972. *Values clarification: A handbook of practical strategies for teachers and students.* New York: Hart.

Smith, C. 1988. Signing naturally: Notes on the development of the ASL curriculum project at Vista College. *Sign Language Studies* 59: 171–182.

Smith, C., E. Lentz, and K. Mikos. 1988. *Signing naturally: Student workbook level 1.* Berkeley: Dawn Sign Press.

Smith, C., E. Lentz, and K. Mikos. 1989. *Signing naturally: Teacher's curriculum guide level 2.* Berkeley: Dawn Sign Press.

Staton, J. 1983. Dialogue journals: A new tool for teaching communication. *ERIC/CALNews Bulletin* 6: 2.

Stokoe, W. C. 1960. *Sign language structure: An outline of the visual communication systems of the American deaf.* Studies in Linguistics no. 8. Buffalo, N.Y.: Department of Anthropology and Linguistics, State University of New York at Buffalo.

Stokoe, W. C., D. Casterline, and C. Croneberg. 1965. *A dictionary of American Sign Language on linguistic principles.* Washington, D.C.: Gallaudet College Press.

Supalla, S. 1986. A manually coded English: The modality question in signed language development. Master's thesis, University of Illinois, Urbana-Champaign.

Supalla, T., and E. Newport. 1978. How many seats in a chair? The derivation of nouns and verbs in American Sign Language. In *Understanding language through sign language research*, ed. P. Siple. New York: Academic Press.

Sutton, V. 1981. A way to analyze American Sign Language (ASL) and any other sign language without translation into any spoken language. In *Teaching American Sign Language as a second/foreign language:*

*Proceedings of the third national symposium on sign language research and teaching*, ed. F. Caccamise, M. Garretson, and U. Bellugi. Silver Spring, Md.: National Association of the Deaf.

Swain, M. 1985. Communicative competence: Some roles of comprehensible input and comprehensible output in its development. In *Input in second language acquisition*, ed. S. Gass and C. Madden. Rowley, Mass.: Newbury House.

Valli, C., and C. Lucas. 1995. *Linguistics of American Sign Language: An introduction*. 2d ed. Washington, D.C.: Gallaudet University Press.

Vigil, N., and S. Wilcox. 1996. A state of the art sign language learning system based on computer videoconferencing technology. Paper presented at CALICO (Computer Assisted Language Learning Consortium), May 27–June 1, 1996, Albuquerque, New Mexico.

Wilcox, K. 1982. Ethnography as a methodology and its application to the study of schooling: A review. In *Doing the ethnography of schooling: Educational anthropology in action*, ed. G. Spindler. Prospect Heights, Ill.: Waveland Press.

Wilcox, S. ed. 1988. Academic acceptance of American Sign Language. *Sign Language Studies* 59: 101–108.

———. 1989. *American Deaf culture: An anthology.* Silver Spring, Md.: Linstok Press.

Wilcox, S., and J. Corwin. 1990. The enculturation of BoMee: Looking at the world through deaf eyes. *Journal of Childhood Communicative Disorders* 13: 63–71.

Woodward, J. 1973. Some characteristics of Pidgin Sign English. *Sign Language Studies* 3: 39–46.

Woodward, J. 1980. Some sociolinguistic aspects of French and American Sign Languages. In *Recent perspectives on American Sign Language*, ed. H. Lane and F. Grosjean. Hillsdale, N.J.: Lawrence Erlbaum.

Woodworth, N. 1991. Sound symbolism in proximal and distal forms. *Linguistics* 29: 273–299.

Wundt, W. 1921. *The language of gestures.* The Hague: Mouton.

# Index

# About the Authors

SHERMAN WILCOX is Associate Professor of Linguistics at the University of New Mexico and faculty member in the Bachelor of Science Degree Program in Signed Language Interpreting. Wilcox conducts research on American Sign Language, fingerspelling, and Deaf culture. His publications include *American Deaf Culture: An Anthology* (Linstok Press), *The Phonetics of Fingerspelling* (John Benjamins), and "The Gestural Expression of Modals in American Sign Language" (chapter in J. Bybee and S. Fleischman, *Modality in Grammar and Discourse,* John Benjamins), and, with his colleagues David Armstrong and William C. Stokoe, *Gesture and the Nature of Language* (Cambridge University Press). Dr. Wilcox is currently general editor of the journal *Evolution of Communication*.

PHYLLIS PERRIN WILCOX, Assistant Professor of Linguistics at the University of New Mexico, is coordinator of the Bachelor of Science Degree Program in Signed Language Interpreting, where she also teaches and supervises practicum students. She currently publishes research articles on semantics and metaphorical mapping in ASL. She has served as a chair of the Registry of Interpreters for the Deaf (RID) National Review Board and was principal investigator of the "Linguistic Training of Signed Language Interpreters" grant awarded by the National Science Foundation to prepare interpreters for the 1995 Linguistic Institute. She received a Modern Language Association fellowship to support her studies in the teaching of ASL as a second language. She served on the RID Task Force to develop the Certified Deaf Interpreter certification process.